CREATIVE IDEAS IN

FLORISTRY

AND

FLOWER ARRANGING

*This foliage and seed head arrangement with its centre comprising a decorative cabbage
is set in Oasis on an antique cake stand. It is made up of:
Dock, Poke Weed, Ladder Fern, Poppy seed heads, Aspidistra, Fatsia Japonica,
Heucherella rubrum, Fennel, Hedera buttercup, Molucella laevis, Elaeagnus,
Helichrysum, Sedum, Timothy grass, Cobaea Scandens, Pelargonium, Berberis,
Geranium crispum, Rose rugosa, Water spiraea, Echevaria.*

Constance Spry

CREATIVE IDEAS IN

FLORISTRY

≈ AND ≈

FLOWER ARRANGING

HAROLD PIERCY

CHRISTOPHER HELM

London

© 1989 Harold Piercy

Line illustrations by David Henderson

Christopher Helm (Publishers) Ltd, Imperial House,
21–25 North Street, Bromley, Kent BR1 1SD

ISBN 0-7470-2612-2 √

Typeset by Opus, Oxford
Printed and bound in Hong Kong

Contents

Short note of thanks

No book of this kind is really written by just one person – it is the people behind the scenes that are so important, yet so often they are left out when it comes to the title and writing about the author. I could certainly not have managed to put together this book without my staff and many friends, who encourage me all the time with the excellent work they produce when teaching the students on our various courses.

Rosemary Jeffcock has done most of the wedding flowers this time, together with some other arrangements, whilst Gayle Derrick has encouraged me with comments and suggestions for what I should add. The lovely two-candle table centre is her work and she also did the swagging over the Christmas fireplace in class, with the help of the students. Philippa Eve and Helen Woodcock made the superb wreaths for me – these really show imagination and charm.

I borrowed the wonderful mixed green on page 76 from my good friend Fred Wilkinson. It was done to show a class he was taking at the time, and I asked that it be left intact. The drawing of the little silver cake top and garland in artificial materials I spotted when Pauline Bellingham was showing student ideas for Christmas decorations. I asked that it be held for David Henderson to copy.

My rough notes were put into a presentable form by Sue Barrett – a terrific job because my thoughts run quicker than my pen can get them down. Susan Carter joined me at the end and her final tidying up and the transferring of the copy onto the word processor has been invaluable.

I am most grateful to Paul Grater for his superb camera work.

There are still many more who have helped by loaning props and I thank them. Finally thanks to the team at Christopher Helm who I hope you will agree have made something worth adding to the range of books on this subject. To help you with the work, within this book you may find it helpful to refer to *The Constance Spry Handbook of Floristry*, also published by Christopher Helm.

The author and publishers would like to thank the following for their assistance in the preparation of the colour photographs:

Osborne & Little   Wall coverings
Ilford   Use of photographs
Barnet Saidman   Use of photographs
West 10 Studios   Use of photograph
Jo Hemmings for help with photography venue.
Annie Grubb for the decorated wedding cake.
Julia Hunter for the cake table garland.

1. Plant propagation

There are very many books covering plant propagation and I do not propose to go into great detail. I will list a number that you may find useful in your studies. The more you know about plants and their growing requirements the better able you are to help your customers. Many new ideas keep coming along to help you with plant propagation. It all takes time to do properly and plants, like children and animals, need regular and careful attention all the time. Perhaps the most helpful advice I can give to you would be to say, do not start too early.

Equipment necessary for plant propagation

A really good knife should be purchased – one with a medium-size blade which sharpens easily and will retain a fine cutting blade to make a clean cut. There are many types of knife about but one with a straight blade and flat tapering handle used in budding will be ideal. Keep it clean, oiled and always have the blade well sharpened to ensure a clean cut.

A good pair of sharp secateurs may well be useful for preparing cuttings of hard wood and the blade of a good spade will often help with the initial chopping up of the plant.

Rooting hormones have been brought out over the last few years to help with callus formation and root development. Different strengths are used for the different cuttings and you should follow the makers' instructions.

A dibber will be most useful for making the hole round the edge of the pot in which to insert the cuttings. These become old friends and last for years. They are made from a piece of wood of pencil thickness upwards.

A can with a fine rose will be needed to water the cuttings in, and settle the soil around the stems. Keep the soil damp to aid rooting. Today there are different forms of 'constant moisture' or mist available. A 'magic leaf' can be used to direct a fine water spray over the cuttings. This plays for a few seconds, to damp the tissue, then cuts out. As the 'leaf' dries out, so it sets the sprays working again. This method prevents wilting of soft tissue and aids rapid rooting of certain plants. A propagation bench is set up as a special climate within the greenhouse. Bottom heat may come from a framework of hot water pipes or electrical cables in the soil of the frame.

A form of 'presser' will be useful in getting the cutting bed prepared. It is important that it is firm and level to hold the right sort of water table.

You will need a range of small and medium pots to hold compost for individual or a small number of cuttings. Shallow and medium depth boxes for root cuttings and half pans are useful although they are not now readily available. These are half the depth of the normal plant pot. I like clay pots rather than plastic pots for cuttings, because more air can reach the root system as they develop.

You should start with a good open sandy compost. In some cases just plain sand will do, but once rooted there is no food value in sand so the 'rooted' cuttings must be potted off into a good medium compost. Always have a layer of dry sand as the top of the cutting bed so that when inserting the cutting, the sand layer drops to the base of the hole before the cutting is pressed in. For everyday use and where cuttings tend to be neglected slightly a mixture of loam, peat and sand will be best and to this end the John Innes Institute have devised a cutting compost of one part medium loan, two parts moist granulated peat and three parts coarse silver sand. No food is added.

Always see that good drainage is available. Some people have a cutting frame: this is a protected area under glass, often within a greenhouse. The area is filled with cutting compost and sometimes bottom heat.

Growing your own plants

Let us start with seed sowing as a good way to grow plants. If all goes well, it is a quick way of producing a large number of plants for bedding out for display or for cutting material. One point to remember: it pays to buy seed of good quality if you expect to produce good plants.

Sowing in boxes is quite a simple process if the following points are observed. First it is essential to have a high-quality compost of good texture, providing an adequate and balanced supply of food which is free from all harmful organisms. There are many composts made but I still feel that the most suitable is the John Innes Seed Compost. The new types seem to be higher in peat content and so much lighter in texture. Perhaps when using plastic pots, which tend to remain rather wet and not able to breath, this is alright but I find them a little too light and airy for most seedlings. John Innes Seed Compost is made up of good loam, moist peat and sharp sand; it retains moisture, yet remains open in texture. Both chalk and plant food are added to allow maximum plant growth.

For best results the compost should be freshly made, so it should be obtained when required from nurseries or garden centres with a big turnover of stock. The seed compost is ideal for seed sowing and the first stages of plant development up to potting in 3½″ pots. Richer mixtures such as John Innes Potting Compost No. 1 should be used for larger pots, and growing on the more vigorous plants. This is made of the same ingredients in different proportions and contains more plant food.

To grow, seeds must be provided with moisture, warmth and air. The art of sowing seeds in boxes or pans is to provide these conditions so that all the viable seeds will start to grow as soon as possible and make good plants. Even germination is important and this will only occur when the right conditions and good quality seed are available.

I like to use a seed box of 2½″ depth and preferably made of wood with good drainage gaps, but today these are difficult to find, so use a good firm plastic seed tray; one that does not bend and crack when filled with soil. There is no need to place broken crockery in the box if a good, open compost is used. Seed beds of a greater depth than 2″ remain cold and wet. The seedlings are not so easy to lift out from the seed bed and waterlogged soil does not contain

Filling up a seed tray with compost,
levelling it off with a straight edge,
then pressing

enough air for good growth. Seed beds under 2″ in depth dry out too quickly. The condition of the compost should be such that when squeezed in the hand it retains its shape but crumbles down when tossed lightly from hand to hand. If too wet, it is sticky to the touch and if too dry it will not form to any mould.

If you work to an organised method you will find it much easier to get a good finish to your seed bed. Have a firm, level table or work bench. Place the box on a flat surface against the heap of compost, draw two to three good handfuls into the box, level and lightly firm the corners and along the box edge (it is this area that tends to dry out first). Then completely fill the seed box, scraping off the surplus compost with a straight edge. Tap each side of the box sharply on the bench three times. This will settle the bottom level of the compost. Firm the top level of the compost with a 'presser' – ideally a piece of wood the size of the box – which has pegs set in its sides, ½″ from the base, to stop it going down too far. This will give an even, level seed bed which is firm but springy to the touch.

The seed should be sown evenly on this surface, allowing equal space for each seed to give ideal growing conditions. If sown too deep they will take longer to germinate; if not sown deep enough the seedlings will fall over after germination, or not grow properly. It is important to sow the right number of seeds in each container. If sown too thickly they may become drawn, if not pricked out at once, and there is a chance of 'damping-off'. If sown too thinly, space is being wasted and fewer boxes or smaller containers could have been used. The optimum number of seeds has not been worked out in detail but it is

Two methods of 'spot sowing'

Left, a seed tray covered with glass and newspaper: right, a seed tray standing in a bowl of water deep enough so that the water just shows on the soil surface

important to give each seed its own living space and avoid overcrowding. If there is a chance that the seedlings may have to remain in the seed bed longer than usual, sow a little less seed.

An idea of seed content to a standard box is 300–400 Tomato seeds or 500 Lettuce. For Lobelia, far more, but when pricking out these should be grown on in little clumps. There are many ways of sowing seeds – direct from the packet, pinch by pinch with thumb and finger from a reservoir of seed in the palm of the other hand, or by running the seed in the palm of the hand tapping it with the other. All these are good ways, but the last is probably the easiest to learn. Keep your hands about 4″ above the seed bed level, so the seed will scatter slightly as it falls. Work across the box area. The deeper a seed is sown the longer it will take to come up even if all other conditions are ideal. Never cover any deeper than necessary. A 3″ flower pot holds just enough soil to cover a standard seed box with ⅛″ of soil. Pass the covering soil through a ⅛″ sieve to get a fine texture. Hold the sieve above the seed beds and pour the soil out evenly, working across the box area. You will get better coverage with compost just a little drier than that used for the seed bed.

The seed box is then watered by standing it in a shallow 1″ tray and allowing the moisture to rise up through the soil. Don't water overhead with a rose on the can as this tends to pan the soil down. Stand the box for a few minutes only – the dampness should not show on the surface. Lift to one side and allow to drain before moving away to the greenhouse. The soil should remain moist enough now to complete germination if the box is covered with a piece of glass. This is then covered with a sheet of newspaper to prevent the air under the glass from getting too hot. Remove the paper as soon as any signs of germination occurs. The glass will come off shortly afterwards.

Pricking out and evenly spacing seedlings from a seed tray

How to handle and plant a seedling. Make a good hole to hold the root area of the seedling. Holding the seedling by the 'seed leaf' in your right hand and the dibber in your left, cover the roots and firm in gently

Pricking out

As soon as the seedlings are large enough to handle they should be pricked out into boxes of the same horizontal dimensions but 3″ deep. John Innes No. 1 may now be used. Handle the seedlings with great care. Lift from the soil by holding the seed leaf and not the stem after carefully loosening from the seed bed with a label. Mark out the new seed box allowing equal space for each seedling usually nine rows by six to a standard seed box 14″ × 9″. Make a hole with a blunt stick of pencil thickness and carefully place the young seedlings in the hole, pressing slightly at the side of the stem with the stick to firm. If using standard sized boxes, a presser with studs in its base may be made to fit the box. These studs mark the soil surface and at each mark you plant a seedling.

A presser, used to create a pattern of holes for 'spot sowing' or pricking out

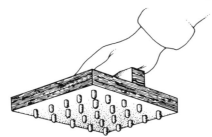

There are many new trays available, one of which is designed like a honeycomb with many little compartments. These are filled with compost and a seedling placed in each. After pricking out, water very carefully to settle, and replace under greenhouse conditions.

A box of seedlings ready to be pricked out

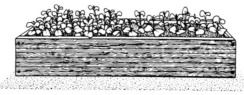

Keep up a good growing atmosphere, allowing plenty of light as the seedlings must not become drawn. Grow up on shelves, gradually hardening off. Some pots may be filled at this time to grow on as plants for inside decorations. Many plants are now potted 'off' from these plant trays into 3½″

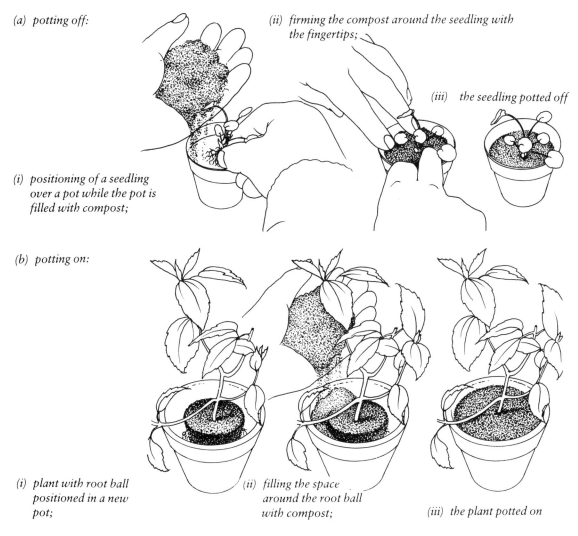

(a) potting off:

(ii) firming the compost around the seedling with the fingertips;

(iii) the seedling potted off

(i) positioning of a seedling over a pot while the pot is filled with compost;

(b) potting on:

(i) plant with root ball positioned in a new pot;

(ii) filling the space around the root ball with compost;

(iii) the plant potted on

pots and then potted 'on' into 5″ pots ready for sale as pot plants. Only a few plants are sold in large pots, these taking much longer to grow and fetching much bigger prices. Only pot on when the ball of soil becomes full of roots. Plants that are over potted look unbalanced and certainly will not move so quickly in your shop. A flowering plant wants just to be showing colour and be full of buds, well balanced and having plenty of healthy foliage.

If plants are to grow well, they should never be checked. If you know that you cannot use them straight from the box, pot off into individual pots where they will grow happily, filling the ball of soil with roots. Feed if necessary, then plant up in window boxes or tubs. The earlier you move seedlings from the seed bed, the less damage there is to the root system. Moving from pot to pot does far less damage to the root system than allowing a seedling to become too large in the box and then trying to pot them off. The root tips are the important part, along with the young root hairs just behind as this is the area where all the growth activity takes place.

Division

This means precisely what it says; that is, the division of the plant into many parts. There are only certain plants that may be divided into several pieces which will grow on into complete new plants. Good examples are Aster (Michaelmas Daisy), Achillea and Chrysanthemum maximum. The subject must be a plant that makes numerous shoots or offsets either above or below ground level. There is more to raising plants from division than you would think. First only propagate those in a healthy condition and producing good flowers true to type. Only take the young healthy growth and not any of the worn-out tissue from the centre of the clump. I often read about dividing with two forks but in doing this you can so easily get dead or worn out material from the centre, which is useless. It is the young healthy growth from the outside of the clump you require.

Division of plants can be sub-divided into various groups:

1. Those plants, such as Michaelmas Daisy, which are naturally spreading and free-rooting. Sub-division may be carried out during late autumn or early spring. It is very easy, with a 100 per cent take.

2. Plants with a more compact nature, such as Delphinium and Lupin. These may be divided if growing well. They must get a little of the fleshy roots or crown. Actually these may be propagated by cuttings also.

3. Groups of bulbs, often with a single stem but with many offsets around this centre portion. In this group are Daffodils and Tulips.

4. Those with creeping roots (Rhizomatous). In this group is the Flag Iris, and certain grasses. Cut up into young pieces they will get away well. These are the modified stems which creep along the ground or just below the surface. It is normal to deal with these straight after flowering.

5. Plants which throw up suckers some distance from the parent plant, for example Raspberries and Willow. These so-called suckers can be most annoying but are a good way of getting new plant material.

6. Tuberous rooted plants such as Potato and Dahlias. One way is to divide up the tubers into sections to produce more plant material. You must select material with a growing point.

Care must be taken in all these groups to get a good healthy piece. Weak, poor-quality material will never make a good plant.

When dividing growths from 'dirty' ground, thoroughly wash the root stock and remove any weed roots which may be matted into the plant tissue you are dividing. Remove surplus or damaged roots by careful trimming. Don't be greedy and divide into too small a clump. It is only the young portion of the plant that you should save to grow on. Plant up straight away in nursery beds, carefully dating and labelling each group of plants.

This is a natural form of propagation carried out in autumn and spring – normally easy to do and with a high rate of success. It is good to divide up plants in the border every four to five years. This keeps up the vigour and allows a thorough cleaning of the beds if they have been allowed to become infested with weeds.

Layering

This is another way of reproducing plants which occurs naturally both in hard and soft-wooded plants. It is the term used to describe the method of rooting branches, stems or runners while still attached to the parent plant, and occurs in trees, shrubs, and small herbaceous plants. Perhaps the best examples are Blackberry and Strawberry, with the Blackberry rooting from its growing 'tip', and the Strawberry with roots occurring at every node of the 'runners'. With trees, it is the friction from constant rubbing of the lower branches on the soil that starts the adventitious roots forming. This is very common in the Rhododendron.

Many plants are raised commercially from layering. Fruit tree stocks and many foliage crops are grown for cutting for market. In treating them this way you obtain straight, clean growth for easy bunching. Willow, Prunus and Cornus come to mind straight away.

Tip layering is a good way to produce young plants. About 2–3″ of the growing point should be buried into sandy soil – sometimes into prepared pots. Peg down if the shoot is very strong and keep the area moist. As soon as growth appears, sever from the main stem but allow to grow on for a few weeks, then lift and plant out in a permanent place. Blackberries, Loganberries and Gooseberries can be grown this way. They will fruit in 2–3 years.

Serpentine layering is done with flowering shrubs growing in situ. Set pots around the base of the plant and peg the shoots into a number of these. Roots will develop from each group of leaves or nodes. Each section of the trailing stem may later be cut up, allowing each plant to develop in the pot of prepared compost. This can be used to increase Clematis and Lapageria. Some people recommend splitting the trailing stem below the leaf joint. Hold the cut surface open and dust with a rooting hormone powder.

Runner production, such as in Strawberries can be prolific. Keep only good, healthy stock and limit the number of plants produced to five or six. Done straight away from fruiting plants which are one or two years old. Peg down the first plants produced from the main stock – again into open ground or prepared pots set around the parent plant.

Pegging down growing branches, such as those of Cornus, which are so decorative in wintertime because of their wood colour, easily produces roots. Just peg down the branches 12–18″ from their growing point. This is usually done in March or September, with the 'plant' often being removed after one year.

Prepare the land around each plant with extra sand and peat, and choose young healthy shoots of good shape. These are cut on the underside, or the branch is twisted, to break the fibres of the stem and expose the cambium layer from which the roots will develop. Layering of Roses (ramblers and climbing) and Lilac may also be treated in this way.

Many of the Carnations coming into the market have young shoots of healthy foliage at their base. These may be rooted quite easily round the edge of a pot. Once growing, the young shoots may then be layered to produce more plants. Border pinks and Spray Carnations make excellent plants for this treatment.

AIR LAYERING   This is an old method of taking a cutting from a plant which has grown out of its useful size, such as the Rubber Plant. Cut round the stem carefully, just below a good growing shoot, and dust with hormone powder. Pack the cut surface with damp moss and cover with a wrap of polythene, bound at both ends to keep the moss damp. If all goes well the roots will fill the plastic pack. Once this has happened sever the plant from the main stem and pot up in a good compost. The young roots will be brittle so pot with care. Once these roots have formed a nice ball of soil, pot on in a richer compost. This method may be used for shrubs growing in situ.

Cuttings

What is a cutting? It is a term used so often in the gardening world, yet what does it really mean? It is, roughly speaking, a portion of the plant and may be in the form of a stem, a root, or a leaf, which is used to grow into a new plant. The most important factor when using any form of material as 'cutting' is to choose healthy growth which is typical of the plant you wish to grow – free from any pest or disease, well ripened (not etiolated, weak or soft) and known to have carried flowers if it is a flowering plant.

IRISHMAN'S CUTTING is the name given to a piece of plant already showing roots or root initials. It is a good way to produce a new plant quickly, that is certain to grow. Take the shoot along with a piece of stem with roots attached. Pot up singly in a small pot or set up the cuttings – 4–5 round the edge of a larger pot if a well-balanced growing plant is required. A good example of this is Tradescantia. Some people prefer to place these pieces of stem first into a small pot of water to get the roots developing before setting up in the soil.

A selection of cutting types:

A   leaf (three types)

B   Heel

C   Softwood

D   Root

E   Vine

F   Tips of foliage (young heather)

G   Hardwood

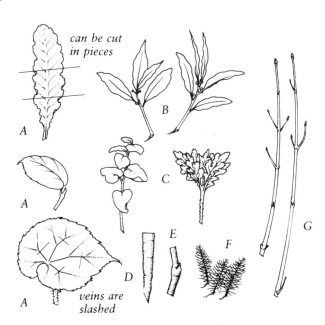

Leaf cutting in gel (left), and placed around the edge of a pot in a ring of sand (right)

HARD WOOD CUTTING These cuttings are normally taken in the autumn, once the leaves have dropped at the end of the growing season. It is important to get well-ripened typical growth – straight pieces of wood from 10–18" long. This is an ideal method for producing shrubs and soft fruit. The soft tip is removed with a clean, slanting cut just above a bud, and a straight cut is made at the base.

The cuttings are set out in nursery rows 4–8" apart, depending on the material. The ground has been prepared and rows of sand drilled where the cuttings will be placed in a shallow drill – the wood being inserted 5–6" deep and well firmed. Keep the rows wide enough apart or keep the bed clear of weeds with constant hoeing.

Rooting should take place during the winter months and the plants may well be ready to move on the next autumn. The addition of hormone rooting powder may help, but many cuttings root easily without it.

HALF RIPE CUTTING This term refers to the condition of the plant tissue. The top of the cutting is not normally cut out – it is a method used with many herbaceous plants when the growing material (well past the soft wood stage) is used to grow on a stock. A good example would be Pentstemon and Geranium. The majority of these cuttings will need protection during the winter – growing in nursery beds or round the edge of pots they develop roots during the winter. Good well-ripened firm material 2–6" long. Always cut with a clean straight cut below a leaf.

SOFT WOOD CUTTINGS These are taken from young growing shoots. They are about 2" long and pencil thickness. The right time is often in the spring, for example, Delphinium and the Chrysanthimum. Take typical growing points – 2–3 from a large plant – and root them to produce new stock.

Soft wood cuttings are best rooted in warm conditions. Cuttings with soft, furry tissue tend to damp off more readily so it pays to reduce the number of leaves on the cutting and to keep them a little dryer. Cuttings with very big leaves may have the leaf surface reduced by half on the older leaves. This cuts down transpiration and drying out.

CUTTINGS WITH A HEEL   This applies mostly to hard wood cuttings. It may be that the plant you are trying to root is difficult and that a little of the older tissue should be left on. This part is called the heel and it should be trimmed neatly. Some growers believe that rooting takes place more quickly from this area.

Rooting of conifer material may be difficult because of the resinous nature of the stem tissue. Those that are a problem need their cuttings to stand in hot water for a short period before inserting in the normal way. The resin, if not soaked from the cut surface, congeals at the base and prevents the callus tissue forming. Abies and Picea are the most difficult.

PIPINGS   Remove basal leaves and cut cleanly at a leaf joint. Then insert in sandy bed. The young shoots of Carnation make ideal pipings – the growing point is not cut but pulled out of the stem tissue. The break should be made at a node. The soft shoots are about 3″ long. Place them round the edge of a pot with a coarse, sandy soil as the rooting medium. You can treat the cut surface with hormone powder to aid rooting.

EYE CUTTINGS   The plant that comes to mind straight away for this method of propagation is the Vine, which is coming more and more into the limelight: Vine growing is taking on in this country. The well-ripened wood is removed in the autumn once the leaves have dropped. It is cut up into units containing a good bud or eye, and these are planted in pots or boxes of soil. The cutting is about 1½–2″ long. A clean cut is made each end and the whole is buried into the sand with the eye uppermost and just showing. Roots will develop from the cut surface. Some growers remove a strip of bark right along the base of the cutting to expose more cambium tissue.

BUD CUTTINGS   These are sometimes included with leaf cuttings. The piece of stem with a good leaf and plump bud is trimmed and inserted into a box of sandy soil or the propagating bed. It is the usual way of increasing Camellia. The half-moon of the wood is pinned down into the soil.

ROOT CUTTINGS   There are two types:
1)   Thick and fleshy
2)   Wire-like threads
The cuttings are taken from the plant in the dormant period. Lift and wash well, then select the material to carry on the plant life. It is a very simple way of increasing the plant stock.
1)   Cut the fleshy roots into pieces 1–2″ long. Make a straight cut at the top, and a slanting cut on the base. Place the cuttings in a deep box – the flat top of the root goes just below the sandy top soil surface. Place in a cool place. The ideal thickness is that of a fountain pen. Plants that will grow in this way are: Statice, Anchusa, Poppy, and Seakale.
2)   Thin wirey roots which are 1–2″ long are laid horizontally on the surface of a box, or in a prepared bed. If they are difficult, you may pin them down with wire hairpins. Then cover with sandy soil. This method may be used for Phlox.

LEAF CUTTINGS Perhaps more interest is taken in this method of increasing plants than any other and, at a guess, the St. Paulia is the most popular plant to illustrate it. There are many leaves which can be used for cuttings. They could perhaps be divided into three types:
1) Small leaves with a short stem.
2) Large flat leaves.
3) Sessile leaves which are cut in sections.
They are all best done in a propagating frame with a little bottom heat. In the open, the root formation is slower and the rotting factor is greater.
1) Small leaves, with short stems, are set up in rows on the sandy soil surface. Can be done in a bed or on the top of a plant pot. The leaf stem is inserted into a hole made with a dibber and pressed well in, so that the basal part of the leaf is in contact with the sandy soil surface.
2) Prepare from well-developed, large, flat leaves. Turn upside-down and make a number of incisions with a sharp knife across the main veins near where they branch. Then lay the leaf down flat on to the sandy compost, mixed well with peat moss to retain the moisture. At the point of the incision, you will find new plant tissue will develop. Eventually the old leaf will fall away. It is better not to pin the leaf but just allow it to lie on the flat surface. This is ideal for Begonia Rex leaves.
3) Leaves which are long and strap-like, such as Streptocarpus, may be cut into sections, discarding the soft tips. It is the basal part which usually roots the best but two or three cuttings can be obtained from each well-developed, large leaf. Place in an upright section round the edge of the pot or in nursery rows. As soon as roots develop from the cut midrib, a small plant will start growing at the base. Pot up separately, and provide bottom heat to get good results.

LILY SCALES This is another way of increasing plant material. The Lily is lifted straight after flowering and scales are removed from the edge of the parent bulb. These are stood upright in boxes of prepared compost with the tips just showing above the soil. The scales will produce small bulbs at their base and, at the same time, one leaf will appear at the growing tip. Leave in the container to grow on – just top dress to build up the compost. Add to this some plant food to help build up the plants.

BUDDING AND GRAFTING These are two specialist methods of plant propagation – interesting to study and fascinating to work. They are a little advanced for many amateurs to handle, so I feel justified in mentioning them without going into detail. Both are forms of propagating which take a longer time to produce an end-product that those already listed and need special growing stocks for taking the buds or grafts. Both also require skill with knife work.

If you are interested in these procedures there are a number of books which cover the work in greater detail. *The Grafter's Handbook* by R.J. Garner is excellent.

Many plants can be raised in different ways – I am just giving you different types of cuttings and methods, so you can try them out for yourself.

Planted copper trough

These plants are all growing and should prove quite long-lasting if planted when just coming into flower. They are set in a good compost and kept damp with spraying overhead from time to time. The foliage plants and stone pieces, moss and gravel are semi-permanent, but the flowering plants are changed all the time to keep up the fresh garden look.

Containers for Planting

There are various containers which lend themselves to a group of growing plants like this. There are some good pieces of copper and brass to be found. If you see any, and they are in good condition, they are worth buying because they are not made now and will never be available again. Any time I use mine I am always asked if I want to sell it. The modern containers do not match them in quality. The copper or brass container is something that I would call a 'long-term' container for growing plants as a decoration. You may start in the late winter and go through to early spring with the small flowering bulbs, then for the summer it is suitable for Fuchsia, Primula or Hydrangea, and in the autumn, mixed-coloured Cyclamen or Begonia, and again, mixed plants around the Christmas period such as Azalea, Solanum and Begonia.

The plants themselves are 'bedded' into the moist soil or peat – one of the composts today with 'perlite' in it are nice and light, and make an excellent medium to hold the plants. One or two foliage plants may become almost permanent, with the flowering plants dropped in when just coming into flower.

Today in the market or your local flower shop, you will be able to buy a large range of flowering bulbs in pots – Crocus, Iris, Snowdrops, Tulips, Aconites, miniature Daffodils, Hyacinth, Snake's Head Lily and Scilia with Polyanthus, Primula and Azalea. These all give excellent results in a garden setting, which you can see illustrated on the preceding pages. In this planting, I have used a large flowered Azalea Miniature Narcissi Hawera, a variegated Ivy, Primrose, two Primula auticula, Anemone pulsatilla, Chionodoxa, Primula denticulata, Heather and a little wild Violet with rock, cork bark, moss the gravel covering the soil surface. The number of plants needed will vary depending on the size of the container, but I would say you require from 6–12 plants to make a show. Let me explain how I planted this up. First select the plants you feel you require. Place them out carefully to get as much interest from them as possible with large at the back down to short ones at the front. Grade for colours and leaf shapes, so that they all go well together. Place some compost in the trough, building the back up a little to get added height. A small amount of charcoal may be added to the base because no drainage will be allowed.

Place one or two of the back ones in position, adding more compost to firm them in, and add some rock to hold them down. Now place the next few plants, more compost to hold them firmly, keeping the soil area a little lower. Now position the front plants, with a little growth over the edge which 'softens' the hard line of the container rim. Keep the soil at different levels and, to add interest, hold it in place with more pieces of rock or cork. Bark, gravel, sand or thick moss can also be used, pinned in place with hairpins made of 22 × 3½″ wires. A pleasing effect can be obtained by using Reindeer moss if green moss is not available, but it is very much more expensive.

Spray overhead to settle the soil and give a damp atmosphere. The plants should have been well watered before planting. Don't get the soil too wet; it should be damp but the plants must not be standing in water. A spray overhead from time to time will help to keep a good growing atmosphere.

2. Window boxes and patios

How many times have you heard people say, 'Oh, I can't grow that because I haven't got a garden'. If care is taken, and this is very important, you can often find a ledge, or an area where some form of plant container can be used, to grow suitable plants. Once you start, your neighbours might follow, thus extending the 'garden' feel to the area.

In my own 'front garden', I have been able to site two tubs, a large antique stone sink garden resting on two sound stone pedestals and a window box. When I first moved to my little terrace home at the side of the Thames I stepped straight out onto bare cobble stones. Never before had I lived in a property without a front garden, so I decided to make a garden by introducing containers that suited the brickwork. At first I wondered whether I would be allowed to do this. Would the Local Council come along and say that the tubs were a hazard to the pedestrians passing by? I decided to develop the garden slowly, and wait and see what happened. I know in certain cases the property is controlled by landlords who have very definite rules and regulations about what can and cannot be done. Then a pleasant request, stating that what you wish to do will add to the decorative content of the property, may well be received favourably.

The window box came first, and I had no real problem getting one as large and as deep as possible to fit securely on the windowsill that looked really good and in the correct proportion. A point worth thinking about today is security; fixing your box at the back, so that it could not be 'lifted', is well worth doing. If the box should overbalance because it was not sitting properly on the windowsill, you would be responsible for any damage done. I have noticed from time to time when travelling by train on entering the outskirts of cities the precariously placed boxes, tin troughs and pots high on window ledges. I am sure that many would not pass the inspection of any surveyor, should he call to check the building. A good stone trough is expensive to purchase so wants looking after carefully.

A wooden tub was the next purchase, intended to hold a pyramid Bay Tree with an underplanting of flowering plants in season. Originally I wanted to tie up with the planting in the trough, but after some fifteen years it now contains a collection of many different plants. The Bay Tree ended up in the river one evening. I was determined to win and planted up again straight away, but with a cheaper type of slow-growing tree and more plants at the base. The tub has since been tipped out a few times but I still persist and now have an altogether better plant collection. Another tub, at the other side, has been added to balance up the setting, together with an excellent old stone sink from a London roof garden. I had to buy two strong pillars on which to support it, and then a collection of plants was added; slow growing, of an alpine nature. It is far too heavy for anyone to attempt to move, so it remains, although the contents are sadly depleted from time to time.

My first big job with the Constance Spry organisation was to look after the plant troughs set up on ledges above the shop windows in Oxford Street as part of the Coronation Decorations. You may well remember that Mrs Spry was brought in by the Minister of Works to advise on the flowers for the Coronation. Part of this job involved the route the coach would take and she came up with the idea of Hydrangeas standing in old ammunition boxes. These were cleverly disguised as only Mrs Spry could do it. She thought up the following idea – remember that materials were very very difficult to come by at and end of the war. After much effort she had some boxes draped with dyed cotton in folds with white cotton ropes and tassels. If the flowers were blue, the swags were red; if the flowers were white, the swags were blue. On some boxes, plaster casts, looking like draped material, were used.

The whole effect was most striking bringing in the red, white and blue effect. The different combinations of box cover and plant changed the pattern throughout the display. The old boxes were so ugly, but could not be seen themselves. They were secured on the ledges, the plants standing in their pots with damp moss or peat around them. If they had been planted in soil they would have been far too heavy. They were maintained by reaching them from the first floor windows – a very precarious and frightening job for me to do because I had to get out on the ledge to reach them. A supply of plants was held in the shop basements and as any showed signs of wilting so they were changed and the sick ones were brought down to recuperate. Hydrangeas 'go down' very quickly once dry but if caught well in time will soon recover. I developed, during the two weeks before the great day, a very keen eye for the behaviour pattern of this particular plant.

In those days window boxes were a novelty. People had gardens to their properties, so were able to grow plants outside. Today many more people rely on plants in boxes, tubs, troughs, and all manner of containers to give colour around the outside of their home. The patio or very small garden have come into their own with modern home design. Land being at a premium has brought this factor home to so many. On some estates the gardens around the houses are managed for the owners so still the individual touch cannot be developed.

There are certain rules which you must follow to get really good results when growing plants in containers, and I recommend that you follow the guidelines below. It is important to have the correct depth to hold the complete ball of soil when planting out.

Drainage is essential – no plants will grow well in waterlogged soil – requiring the correct compost. Any old garden soil is useless. Over the drainage holes some broken crock or roughage should be placed first, then one of the recognised composts. On to this firm base stand the ball of soil, if using pot plants, covering with at least 1″ of compost over the top while still leaving enough space for watering. If planting from a seed box, again fill the box to the required depth then make a hole to drop in the young plant, firming it lightly

Autumn vase arrangement

An upright pottery vase from Holland contains this fairly wide range of cultivated and wild materials. To steady the balance (actual) I have half-filled the container with gravel before adding wire netting to hold the woody stems.

before topping up and levelling off the soil. Remember: the firmer the potting or planting out, the slower the growth of the young plant.

Water in carefully to settle the plant. Keep sprayed overhead to keep a moist atmosphere around the foliage but encourage the young roots to go in search of moisture. Always water the plant well before planting it out, then keep it a little on the dry side without allowing it to wilt, for a few days.

If attempting to use a flat roof, as my neighbour has done, there is no way round it but to use containers, and then check out the structure for weight and evenly distribute containers. It would perhaps be safer to get advice on how much the roof will carry before taking tubs or pots up there. These containers are heavy when full of soil. This is something you must remember if you are a florist when the garden department is asked to make a garden other than on ground level. I have spent many a day lugging sacks of compost on to roof gardens.

Gardening with different-shaped raised beds and containers can be very attractive if well designed. You must remember that these areas will dry out very easily, being only small units of soil. Protection from wind and sun will be necessary and some form of irrigation will be well worth installing. You may wish to have some permanent plants and add extra colour by adding small areas of short-term planting, or you may wish to work to a system where the whole layout is changed at regular intervals – a rather more expensive way to run the garden. One nursing home garden was done in this way, so that all the upstairs rooms looked out on to a garden with maximum colour. You cannot rush at a garden of this kind. Look carefully at it and decide what features are to be incorporated, then on a piece of paper work out a plan. Always remember that when grown well, plants take up more room than you expect. With controlled watering and feeding, which may easily be included, you will get excellent growth. Good-quality containers are well worth the extra money in the first instance. I like fibre glass; it has that lead look and lasts so well. Heavy stone or terra pots are also excellent. Wood can deteriorate quite quickly unless it has a lining. You must have a hard wood – soft woods are useless after a very short period.

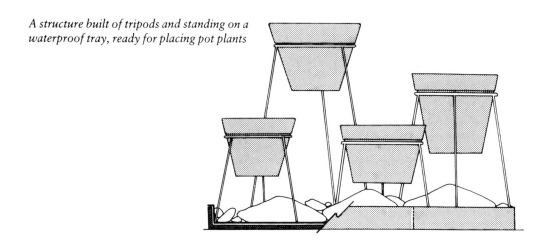

A structure built of tripods and standing on a waterproof tray, ready for placing pot plants

By having your garden in pots you can change the design as quickly as you like. From choice I would prefer to have some permanent raised beds, around the outside area, then have different tripods and interesting containers on the stone floor which can be moved at will to add interest and make clear space when needed. If I could, I would certainly introduce water – that movement does something and the sound of it falling from a ledge of rock has a very soothing effect. If you have introduced different levels then a small pool from the high ground running through an interesting channel to a larger pool at a lower level will be a great joy.

Notes on cone-shaped terracotta pan on a stand

There are many containers available today that can be used to grow Alpines and small herbaceous plants. One which I have found very successful is a fairly shallow terracotta cone shape standing on a metal tripod. The very deep terracotta pots appear ugly to me but those that are about 8–9″ deep at the centre are ideal. First soak your container, if it is new, then carefully drill a good drainage hole in the base. Once this is done, you are ready to proceed with planting.

I would suggest that you first place a fairly large piece of crock over the drainage hole then a few more smaller pieces and on top of that ½″ of gravel. This ensures that the drainage is well catered for. Next you can add a little roughage and then your compost. I find that all I need is John Innes Potting Compost No. 1 and after a while I just top dress with additional plant food, old compost and sometimes one of the proprietary artificial manures.

Select your plants, bearing in mind shape, colour and flowering time. As the container is round, you will have your taller material to the centre and then spreading to the outside. Plants will grow quite quickly, so do not be

A cone in a tripod, shown in section: left, showing the basic contents (with stones below the compost, for drainage); right, after planting. There is a large drainage hole at the bottom of the cone.

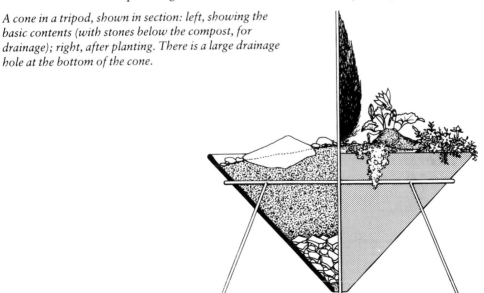

over-generous with your planting. Some material, such as miniature bulbs will die down and other plants can take their place. If evergreen, they will require space; if deciduous, the bulbs may well come up through them and die down before they take over. You must get a balance without overcrowding.

If you are adding any rock or stone, place this first and perhaps a dwarf-growing conifer. Get this well placed and firm, now add more stone to help hold it and weigh down the dish. Firm the plants in: those needing well drained positions can have some sand and small stones placed round them. Once the plants are firmly in position, add more soil and gravel leaving a shallow rim to the container. Do not plant on a mound. Water well in and allow the soil to settle. In a few days you may need to add a little more top soil and a piece of cork bark, sand or stone for added interest.

Watch for weeds; they should be removed straight away. Keep plants growing slowly, and do not allow them to dry out. When well established, you may need to cut back bits to keep them in trim. These make the most attractive small gardens and will go on for years.

Plantings from late autumn onwards

1) Mixed foliage such as Ivy, Acuba, Baby Hebe, Cupressus, Euonymus, Solanum capsicastrum for colour, and winter-flowering Heathers. Early bulbs may be planted at the same time which give colour in January and February. The medium-sized flowers, placed in groups look lovely.

2) Remove many of the above and plant groups of pot-grown bulbs in amongst the evergreens (Solanum, flowered bulbs and Heather come out). The last two items to be grown on for another year.

3) For this next planting remove all the plants in boxes and replant with pots of Hyacinths, and Forget-me-Nots between, or mixed Polyanthus or Pansies. The latter two should certainly be added to the other empty spaces. These colours tend to be very bright but by careful selection you may be able to get individual groups of certain colours together.

4) Groups of Cineraria make a good splash of colour and, to soften the hard edge of the window box, a trailing Ivy can be added. The short multiflora Cineraria plants are the best and quite long-lasting. Some people plant Cyclamen but I never see these as an outside crop except for the charming miniature ones which no garden should be without.

You may wish, by now, to introduce mixed planting so small pots of bulbs. (Short double Tulips or late Narcissi could go in with Primula and more foliage plants). Don't change the Ivies. An expensive plant is the Hydrangea but one or two of these would add interest.

As you can see there is no stopping once you get into growing tubs and boxes provided you have a protected area. The cold winds do the damage. The permanent troughs can be topped up with a few choice alpines now because this is the time they are in the market (April–May).

If you are in a town, or an industrial area, it is no good trying to grow the true alpines such as Gentian because to do well they need pure air. But many of the more common so-called Alpines will give a good display.

5) Now we are into the summer planting which should take place at the end

of May to the end of June, depending on the area in which you live. It is no use starting too early – plants will be checked by the cold and then they are spoilt. Wait until the weather is warmer and plant up.

I believe the commercial traders do more harm than good by putting their plants on the market too early. First-time buyers are so disappointed when they spend their money only to loose their plants later. Once put off they so often do not try again so an on-going potential customer is lost. On the other hand our weather pattern does not help. In fact, no two years seem the same, but I would suggest you leave planting to a little later if in any doubt.

The summer boxes, troughs and hanging baskets can really carry any quick-growing, sun-loving plants provided there is enough room for them. Remember, flowering is encouraged more when plants are not 'over-fed'. Too much plant food encourages a lot of green growth early, then flowers and seeds occur only for the plant to die. You need to aim for the middle of the road, with good healthy growth, then flowering for a long period. Some of the ideas customers get hold of are unbelievable. For instance, I have been asked such things as if by giving double the amount of food, will the plants grow twice as fast? This in fact could result in the plants being killed. One should always tell customers to read the instructions carefully. Modern chemicals are very strong and effective. At one time a bag of manure or soot in a tub of water was fine and provided the 'colour' was right one could do little harm. This is not so today.

I mentioned sun because most annuals are originally from places like South Africa where sun plays a big part in their lives, so you should consider open sunny sites for growing them. One plant that has become very much in vogue is the 'Impatiens', 'Balsam' or Busy Lizzie. This will do well in partial shade and makes a good plant in containers. I have grown it in the last two years in my north-facing window box. One problem I find is that it is necessary to keep removing the dead flower heads. As they drop, they seem to stick on the foliage and look untidy. There are now some excellent colours in this plant and they make a wonderful bright splash under painted shady areas. Go through the seed catalogues and note the new varieties coming out each year – it is worth trying some of these in your small garden.

Another point to remember is that your patio area or small garden may be used in the evening for entertaining. There is nothing better on the right night than to have drinks or a meal outside, so sweet-smelling flowers should be added to your list. Nicotiana in green, white and crimson are so good and they open in the evening.

Remember that herbs will also add to your garden scents, and also provide decorative growing in a large pot which is well drained and in a sunny setting. The use of herbs today has very much come back into vogue, so you have an excuse for adding them to your plant list. Some people try to grow them as a decoration in the kitchen but they are better grown outside. They will grow more quickly and supply more material for cutting. With constant picking and trying to grow under poor conditions inside you will find you are fighting a losing battle. In the winter time a pot of chives, parsley and mint is well worth trying but for many it would be better to have a herb pot made up of small bunches of dried herbs.

Remember, if planting anything like Mint or Horseradish, have them in a controlled bed, such as an old sink in the ground with drainage in it. This stops creeping stems from spreading. Some herbs are very decorative and, although perhaps not much use in cooking, are ideal foliages for cutting to add to the small arrangements.

I have already mentioned water gardens. Remember you want it in the open rather than near trees, where it is too shaded and subject to being filled with fallen leaves each year. The only real problem I have come up against is my four-legged friends – they can be a real nuisance fishing if the pool is too small or the fish too friendly! It does not matter what you have as a pet; fish coming to the surface for regular feeding are easy prey. Protective nets are available but they do tend to spoil the decorative qualities of the whole area.

I am not keen on the idea of introducing vegetables into a very small garden. Today one can so easily buy all sorts of vegetables in small amounts – the supermarkets are always introducing new lines. The amount of crop you get from the odd plant you could perhaps find room for is so small that it is not worthwhile. However, if you have a large garden, then many of the plants can be decorative when growing, so serve a useful dual purpose. I was interested recently to see an old student of mine talking on television about his decorative vegetable garden. Perhaps some things that I have said in the past have rubbed off!

Trees and Plants for troughs, tubs and sink gardens

TREES

Thuja Rheingold	Chamaecyperis obtusa nana
Pinus mugo	Picea mariana
Juniperus sky rocket	Salix boydii
Juniperus communis compressa	Salix montana
Juniperus squamata meyeri	Salix retusa pyrenaica

PLANTS

Miniature Roses	Sempervivum
Primula	Sedum
Saxifraga	Phlox douglassii
Campanula carpatica	Aster alpinus
Veronica	Ameria – Thrift
Dryas	Thymus
Dianthus	Weigela nana variegata
Limonium minutum	Potentilla abbotswood
Anemone Pulsatilla	Alyssum montanum

Something that is not new, but in vogue at present, is the garden growing in a glass case of some description. These gardens make very good decorations and need little attention. They are almost self-watering from the condensation which collects on the glass. There are different designs available, some quite

A fern garden in a glass case

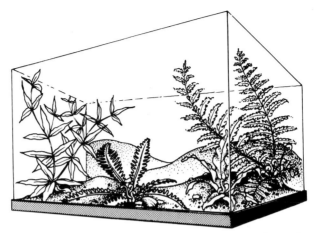

elaborate but all based on the Victorian terrarium or plantarium. They are excellent for many of the slower-growing green plants, ferns, mosses, Saint Paulias, Orchids and insectivorous plants. The beauty of these containers is that they control the atmosphere around the plant whatever happens in the room outside. So often, with modern heating and double-glazing, the plants become too dry around the leaf surface area. Within the glass case a humid micro-climate builds up which suits many of the plants very well. The exchange of gases also works well. A balance is set up by the plants absorbing oxygen and giving off carbon dioxide at night, with the reverse happening in the daylight.

Some people still have the traditional glass domes, but I find these rather fragile and prefer to use them with an arrangement of hand-made or dried flowers.

Another piece of useful equipment is a fish tank. These containers have an advantage over the bottle garden, which can be difficult to control when things go wrong, unless the neck is large enough for you to get your hand through. Once any disease such as the fungus botrytis (grey mould) starts on any dead or dying tissue it spreads rapidly so must be checked straight away. This is the sort of thing that happens when a flowering plant drops its old flowers and starts to decay on the soil surface. Perhaps there is something to be said for only having green non-flowering plants in this environment.

I believe there are certain things one should do when planting up and this will help the plants to get established.

1)   Have a layer of crock and charcoal in the base – about 1″ – with a small layer of clean gravel over the top. This is then covered with a layer of damp peat.
2)   Use a good compost – free from weed seeds. John Innes No. 1 or 2, freshly made, is ideal. This will hold plant food for some time, and later you will feed again.
3)   Next carefully place about 4″ of soil over the bottom and at the same time set in the pieces of interesting shaped rock or stone. Some people like to include pieces of bark, but fungus may develop and cause trouble, so if you use it keep an eye on it.

4) Try to get different levels in the soil surface because this makes for more interest and a better decoration.

5) If you are using a round bowl, such as a large glass-fish type, get your tallest plants in the centre, working to the low ones on the outside.

6) Place out your plants to get different shapes and colours next to each other so that they show up well – just as you would do when doing a mixed green arrangement. There is so much in common with arranging and planting.

7) Prune back plants when they start to get too large. It is a good idea to take cuttings, and then when these are rooted, to remove the old plants and replace them with a more balanced one.

8) Keep a look out for pests and disease. Check straight away if you see anything, and act on it.

I believe that all flower shops should have something for children. It is so important to get young people interested in growing things at an early age. People may not realise that Constance Spry herself was a Head Mistress of a school in the East End of London, not starting with flowers commercially until she was well into her middle age. She was a wonderful teacher, always taking flowers from her own garden into school to show her young pupils, thus getting them interested in new things. Once she had their interest, she could teach them anything.

There are often latent talents in the juniors and once these are sparked off you never know how they may develop. Constance Spry loved her days in the East End with her pupils, and was determined to show them all the beauty that they were missing. As a child she was encouraged by her own father to find and learn about wild flowers, which she loved. So she, in turn, thought it a good idea to try and help her large, deprived school family. I remember well as a child growing a collection of cacti, and these curious plants are a good way of raising young people's interest.

Planting a trough:
top, crocks in position over the drainage holes; centre, a layer of well-rotted manure or garden compost; bottom, the trough filled with compost and planted

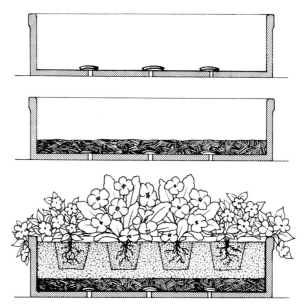

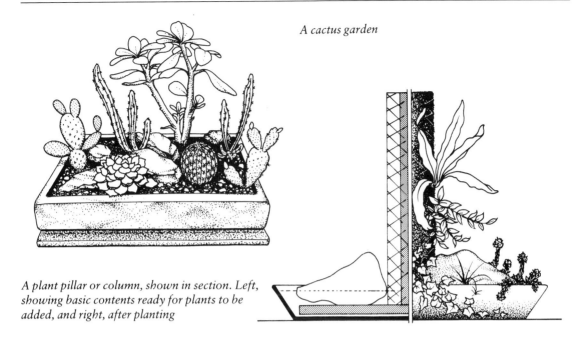

A cactus garden

A plant pillar or column, shown in section. Left, showing basic contents ready for plants to be added, and right, after planting

I have been using hyacinth glasses for years, but something which really gave me many hours of pleasure was, for want of a better name, a 'column of green plants'. It was constructed by using a tube of fine-mesh wire netting secured to a large saucer-shaped dish at the base. This had rocks set in the soil to balance it and some very pretty mosses, Ivy and Sellaginella. The tube, or column, was filled with very open peaty compost mixed with some charcoal. Filling from the top, gradually little plants were tucked in through the wire netting at stations around the tube. There are a number of mosses, small-leaved house plants, and small ferns that will grow well in places like this. After filling the tube with soil and planting up the outside wall of the column, fill in the gaps between the plants with bun moss. Hold it in place with hairpins going through the netting into the soil. Water well, and give a fine spray over the leaf surface.

To get it established, make a tube of fairly thick, clear polythene sheet to go over the column. Once established, keep it damp in the column and well sprayed outside. It will go on for a very long time. One year I added some Crocus to the top and round the base, and these did really well.

The flower trade is always looking for people to join them. Why not try and 'sow the seed' at a young age? Once the interest is there you may get that extra pair of hands on a Saturday and it will develop from there.

Plants for Column

Ficus radicans	Columnea	Cocos
Small-leaved Ivies	Venus Fly Trap	Cryptanthus
Begonia masoniana	Sundew	Pilea
Saxifraga sarmentosa	Begonia boweri	Maranta

3. Pot plants

*A*ny soil, or compost, only acts as a medium in which the root system may run and form an anchorage for the plant so that it may remain upright. Provided this anchorage, plus moisture and some plant nutrients, are provided the young plant will grow. You see this when planting bulbs in shingle: the good bulb has plant nutrients in a large enough amount at its base to enable it to grow and flower. It just requires moisture to get root action and the movement of the cell sap to start the bulb growing.

After flowering you should add plant food to build up the scales of the bulb so that it may flower again the next year. This is hydroponics and this type of culture, in a modified way, is carried on in many systems today.

Potting 'off' and potting 'on' are two terms which you should understand. Young plants (maybe rooted cuttings) are lifted very carefully from the nursery bed having been well watered first so that as much soil as possible stays with the root system. These are potted off into their first pot, which may be 3″ or 3½″ (a small or large 60). Today, with the use of different materials, pots vary in size and number. Originally the No. 30, 48 or 60, for instance, was the number of pots from a given cast of clay. Some pots had large rims; others did not. With a good compost no drainage is used today, but for extra drainage a little crock and gravel may be added to the base of the pot. On to this goes a little compost. Then, working with the prepared compost heaped up on the back of the bench, you place the pot in front of it, and holding the rooted plant in your left hand, place it carefully into the pot. Keeping the main stem to the centre, carefully rest on the bed of soil, and heap round fresh compost with the right hand, turning the pot as you do so, with the soil banked up level with the rim of the pot. Tap the pot on the bench to settle, and press down with two fingers from each hand to firm (thumbs give too much pressure). The firmer you pot, the slower the growth will be, so soft, succulent plants are lightly potted, and woody material in general should be potted on the firm side. Stand out and water lightly to settle in, but do not get too wet. The compost should be fairly damp to start with, and the young root hairs should go out in search of moisture.

Potting on is the term used for potting from a small pot to a larger one. As already stated, if food and water are available in the right amounts, repotting is not necessary except from a visual point of view. A very large plant in a small pot looks very silly and the plant would tend to be unstable and liable to fall over. Some plants are not happy in too large a pot, and only those that grow quickly need potting on and on. Potting on needs to be done at the start of the growing season, normally as days get longer and warmer in the spring. Look at the compost; it may be very poor in texture. Look for roots at the base of the pot and, when knocked out of the pot, if the roots are all matted into a tight ball, this is a sign of the need for potting on. Choose your compost and prepare a heap of it mixed and ready, so that it is just moist enough to stay in one piece when squeezed yet falls apart when touched.

Again, get your clean pot – normally the next size up the scale – and put one piece of crock in the base, a little gravel then a little soil. This should bring the ball of soil up to the correct height in the new pot. Stand the plant in the pot, hold and turn with the left hand and fill with the right hand. Tap well and firm with your fingers. Do not water at this point because the ball of soil should have been moist before potting on. Spray to keep a moist atmosphere. Wait a few days before watering so that the roots are going out into the new soil in search of moisture. Keep your plants growing at a steady rate. Do not allow them to become drawn from lack of light. To keep them a good shape, turn the pots around from time to time. Cut away any dead or damaged parts and watch out for any pest or disease, treating straight away to keep in check. Tie any untidy growth into a stake straight away as it is never easy to stake a plant once it has gone over. This applies when growing both inside and outside.

A few ideas with pot plants in the home

In most cases pot plants look better grouped together than on their own. It helps to make a bold eye-catching display and at the same time any minor defect with one plant is hidden. The plants themselves will do better; they create their own atmosphere which helps with their growth. The different shapes and colours of the foliage make a good contrast and look well in the modern home. Arrange your group where it can be seen but does not get in the way. Keep it away from any radiators and any draughts.

A plant tray is an excellent idea, worked out by Constance Spry many years ago. The plants are all in pots, some of which are arranged on tripods to get the different heights. The rest are stood in-between the legs of the tripod to make use of the room on the tray. There is a layer of pebbles on a tray base to hold moisture. From time to time, to add extra colour and interest, a stem or two of some special plant is set in a plastic tube hidden between the pots.

A plant trough can be treated in the same way but the narrow shape does not allow such an interesting 3-D effect. A plant tray, with a layer of gravel, is perhaps the most simple holder and so easy to arrange. It allows for frequent changes. The problem is when it is not deep enough to hide the pots, so the front plants must be well established with good trailing foliage.

Pot plant care

I believe pot plants are more popular today than ever before and naturally, because of the interest in them, more and more plants are grown for sale in pots. Many people have flats and no garden space, so the only living material they can grow is in a pot.

There is, in many people, an urge to grow plants as opposed to having cut flowers which are quite expensive and last for such a short period. House plants can bring life and colour into the home and, with a little care and attention, remain with us for a long period. They certainly do something to the atmosphere of the home and immediately bring it to life but, like everything living, they will need a little attention and, to obtain the best from them, certain rules and requirements must be studied.

All the plants we wish to grow in our homes will be in conditions far from those really suited to them in real life. They will have started life from a small seed, bulb or cutting and it will be a struggle for them all the time to survive, but in most cases the plant will struggle on.

Life in the nursery will be strict and controlled, and everything will be treated the same; there will be many of the same 'family' being grown. If starting in the home environment it may be a different type of environment and far from the ideal. Theplant may be over-handled and sometimes this is worse than being slightly neglected. Growing commercially in a batch will mean that feeding, watering, and pest and disease control will be automatic and the special needs of the individual will not be studied. By this treatment the plant will be somewhat hardened off to make it more ready for its unnatural existence in the sitting room; learning to adapt is very important for all plants.

Plants can adapt in many ways and so much more detail about this subject has been brought home to us by television programmes during the last few years. Trying to follow nature as far as possible is what you should aim to do.

Why do plants not succeed? So often people will ask me what they did wrong. You may be able to pin the trouble down straight away or it may be rather complex, but here are a few points to think about.

OVER WATERING   I would suggest that this is probably the most serious of all plant troubles. People tend to think a plant always needs a drink irrespective of the conditions. Roots in very wet soil become 'drowned' and then do not function properly. This in turn gives way to unhealthy foliage and, in a very short time, the plant will cease to function, and die. On first looking at the plant, it may appear to be wilting from lack of water, but on feeling the compost or lifting the pot you will immediately find it is very heavy and the soil sodden. The leaves may well be turning yellow and soft to the touch.

NOT ENOUGH WATER   On the other hand, lack of water will in turn cause the plant to wilt and the foliage to turn brown and shrivel up. In a greenhouse you can determine a good growing atmosphere but in the house this is more difficult. A spray of fine moisture over the leaf surface from time to time will work wonders.

DRAUGHTS   A cold draught can be very damaging for certain plants – Cyclamen and Poinsettia come to mind straight away. Plants in the open can get burnt up from the wind and, to avoid drying out in the very cold, they tend to wilt. This checks transpiration from the leaf surface. Also in the cold, the root action is slower and growth rate is cut right back. This in turn checks the movement of water and plant food through the stem and leaf tissue.

SUDDEN TEMPERATURE CHANGE   Changes in temperature which are sudden are not good for plant growth. The plant can tolerate a gradual movement up and down the scale. This is why it is recommended that plants should not be placed on window ledges at night, with a thick blanket of curtain keeping the warm air from the heated room from reaching them while on the other side is the cold expanse of frozen glass. Take your plants in to the room at night.

DRY AIR In many modern homes today, with efficient central heating, the atmosphere is very dry. It is not good for your plants or furniture. Try to keep your plants away from the heat of the radiator and also spray over with a warm mist each day. It keeps the foliage clean as well as moist. Also by standing the pots in damp peat or gravel you create a micro-climate and this in turn will help a lot.

A guide to plants for house decoration

For permanent effect foliage plants with smooth, fairly thick leaves are generally the most satisfactory. Softer plants, such as Coleus and flowering plants can be used in their season to give added colour. They will not last so long, so plant to replace them with other plants as necessary.

The positioning of plants in rooms should be given careful consideration. Windows facing east, north and west are suitable for most plants but plants in south windows should be shaded with light curtaining during the middle of the day on bright days from May to mid September. Plants with green foliage should be used in north-facing windows. Few plants will tolerate the light conditions in the interior of a room unless there is a considerable area of uncurtained window facing south-east, south or south-west. Fluorescent lighting during normal daylight hours has been used successfully on plants in the interior of a room. No plant should be stood directly over a radiator of any type without the installation of a moisture tray.

House plants sent to market and retail distributors are grown in greenhouses and care is necessary in acclimatising them to room conditions. In order that plants shall suffer as little shock as possible, it is advisable to buy from the end of May to the end of August when conditions during transport, in markets and shops are nearer the normal growing conditions than at other times. Plants selected should be sturdy, without drawn straggling growths, and furnished with healthy leaves to the base of the plant.

Plants may be divided into three main groups:
1) Those which will grow in unheated rooms or rooms with occasional heating, such as Hedera and Ficus pumila.
2) Those which will grow in rooms that are kept at above freezing point, rooms with slow burning grates for example. These include Tradescantia, Begonia and Maranta.
3) Those which need a warm room (usually one with central heating). The range of plants for such a room is limited only by the temperature to which the room will fall in cold weather and the moisture in the atmosphere.

The windows in rooms in which plants are grown should be heavily curtained or covered by thick blinds when cold conditions exist outdoors during hours of darkness. As even a temperature as possible should be maintained in rooms in which plants are grown.

The main causes of ill health and death of indoor plants are faulty watering, draughts, and bad atmospheric conditions while serious damage may be done by pests and diseases.

A plant should not be given water at the roots until the soil in the pot is almost dry. The old method of ascertaining this is by tapping the pot with a stout stick or a metal rod. A ringing sound indicates that water is needed. This only applies to uncracked clay pots, which are not used so much today. With plastic pots, less water is used because they dry out less. Soil colour, smell and the weight of the pot will give you the clue to watering. Watering should be done either by filling the space at the top of the pot with water from a can with a spout, or by steeping the pot in water to the rim until moisture appears on the surface of the soil. With the exception of a few plants which like bog conditions, such as Cyperus, pots should never be allowed to stand permanently in water. Water will be needed more frequently in bright, hot weather and plants should be kept fairly dry, but not parched, when growth is slow during winter.

Draughts should be avoided especially when outdoor temperatures are low. Windows as well as doors should be fitted with draught excluders. Windows should not be opened when the outside temperature is below that of the room. The atmosphere in any but a damp house is too dry for really healthy plant growth during spring, summer and autumn, and ideally plants should be stood over troughs of water or on trays of sand, gravel or weathered coal ash kept moist. This is particularly necessary where central heating is installed.

Fumes from gas appliances are injurious to most pot plants and many plants should not be grown in rooms with gas fires unless there is adequate ventilation. Atmospheric pollution, especially in the neighbourhood of factories, often makes for extreme difficulty of cultivation and frequent cleaning of the foliage by spraying or sponging is necessary. The most effective cleanser is probably a white oil insecticide, such as Volck.

Probably the most useful all-round insecticide is liquid derris and a good control for mildew is dipping in 2oz of washing soda dissolved in a gallon of water.

When plants have filled their pots with roots, they will need potting in the next size up. John Innes Potting Compost, or one of the newer types which can usually be obtained from local garden sundriesmen, can be used for most plants. When in active growth, feeding with a complete plant food should take place once a fortnight.

Basket of spring flowers

This arrangement is done in a lovely, deep wicker basket with a fairly low handle. It is oblong in shape but with rounded ends. I first lined it with a black plastic bag, then set a large bowl in the left-hand side, wired up with a piece of Oasis at the back to hold the branches. On the right-hand side I set the pots of Polyanthus plants and small plastic cream cartons for the bunches of Snowdrops and the Lenten Roses. In the left-hand front area I used one variegated Ivy and the sprays of Mahonia Japonica were again in a small cream carton.

The cut foliages and flowers were Viburnum Tinus, Forsythia, Cornus Mas and Hazel Catkin, with a few trails of variegated and dark-green Ivy and the odd piece of Larch.

The flowers were Daffodils, Narcissi – Soleil d'or and primo, dark and pale blue Hyacinth, and Snowdrops. The whole surface area was covered with moss to hide the mechanics.

4. *Making the right choices*

The individual touch

Here you have a very wide choice because no two homes are alike and everyone has their own ideas on what makes a home. You are expressing yourself through your flowers, just as an artist does so with his or her painting.

It is strange, but there are people who, to your eyes, get things just perfect and there are those who miss the boat every time.

The late George Foss, who was with Constance Spry for very many years, was a great home builder. I believe that he moved house around a dozen times in the period that he was with the organisation, and each time he had made a most superb garden and the house was always a dream – so comfortable and 'lived in', and every corner full of interest. Another wonderful home and garden belongs to Sheila Macqueen, a great friend of mine and one who has done so much to foster the name of Spry and to encourage millions with their decorating through her writing and television work. Many of you will have had the chance to visit Sheila's lovely home and garden when it is open to the public. Nobody realises just how much magnificent work Sheila and her friends have done over the years for fund-raising for various charities. Sheila was fortunate to start her career in flowers with Constance Spry herself, and covered the world on lecture tours in the early days.

Many people join us at Winkfield Place, either on a day's visit or for a longer period, and all seem to talk about the atmosphere and the interest around the home. These home-makers somehow have just the knack for finding the right thing for the right place, and the addition of some lovely flowers sets everything off. Your flowers must be part of the overall decoration and in no way should they stand out and jar as you enter the room. For party-time they may be larger and somewhat more exotic because you want that extra effect on these occasions. One occasion I remember well was the problem of the flowers in Westminster School Hall for the Queen's guests after the Coronation. Mrs Spry and her colleagues came up with the idea of clashing reds against the grey stone walls and a gold 'leather' look on the food tables. The tables, with their pale blue cloths and crowns of red flowers in the centre, finished off with the garland of gold leaves below the vase stands, were most striking.

For everyday living and with all the other expenses you have to cover, I like to aim for one small vase of flowers for my dining room and sitting room, the other rooms, unless I have guests with me I tend to leave bare of flowers but do have the odd plant about. I must admit to a couple or so of groups of artificial plants on my landing, which will not allow fresh plant life because of lack of light. I have what I feel is an interesting staircase with three landings and these artificial groups look good here. People using the stairs carefully pass by without looking too closely, and as I have been asked on one occasion for a cutting they cannot be too bad!

For everyday flowers, you will aim for small to medium simple vases, that hold flowers well. There are many of these about if you look around but watch the glaze on some pottery and any 'seconds' on offer should be left well alone. A fault in the glaze can spell disaster. Really all you require is something living, and simplicity. Each year when the cut Hyacinths come from market you often find little sideshoots, flat against the main stem, and showing no colour. These, if carefully pulled away and placed in deep water for a few days, grow into something resembling the Roman Hyacinths we used to get from France before Christmas and into the early part of the New Year. They are wonderful. They make the prettiest of small table bowls and last a really long time. There is never a time when you cannot find something in the garden to add a little personal touch to your home. A normal bunch of those mixed-up flowers and colours coming over from the Continent are not for me. All I want is just a simple rose or spray of Singapore orchids.

I have a secret wish that has amused people at one or two demonstrations. How I long for a 'motorway maintenance' sign. So often I am passing along where I dare not stop and I see the most perfect stems of weeds, or flowers, for instance Cowslips. Then I see one of those vehicles with a 'motorway maintenance' sign standing there with no one about. A Cowslip would probably mean nothing to them! But, thinking again, perhaps if everyone was like me there would be no cowslips by now. Have you noticed how they have increased since we have not been allowed to stop and pick them? Do not think I would go raiding the countryside – all I want it just one or two stems, carefully picked. I have every necessary piece of equipment in the car to look after the cut materials.

Backgrounds and room interiors

As with all sorts of displays, the background can make a very big difference to the overall picture. This is something that has been brought home to me on many occasions and I believe that it is most important before ever suggesting any form of decoration to go and see the place first. Look at it carefully and then choose the sensible places to decorate. Colour is very important and this subject was something very dear to Mrs Spry. She was not afraid in any way to use it but – and I have used the word before – it had to be 'suitable'.

When decorating in a private house, if the rooms have any personality at all you will let this control your plans. So often there will be some feature on which to build the flower scheme. It may be the curtains, carpet or the soft furnishing. Rich colours often look well in a book-lined or wood-panelled room – reds, terracotta, bronzes and yellows. These seem to associate well with the bindings, and more elaborate vases can be used to good effect. In the sitting room of an old cottage, it is the simple garden flowers that look best arranged in tin-lined brown wicker baskets, pewter measures or copper and brass utensils. It would be here that wild flowers in rough pottery containers would look so at home. I have a record of Constance Spry talking when she says 'You do not hang gingham curtains in a gilded salon nor would you use brocade in a country cottage – let suitability be your watchword'.

A natural background and free areas are always the best settings for groups. Never cover up anything with material to hide it – it only makes it stand out like a sore thumb. There are occasions when a vase of flowers on a pedestal may help to hide something that may appear unsightly. This is the sort of problem you find when decorating the village hall. So often those soulless, purpose-built buildings have few decorative properties. Groups of flowers usually look best when set against the solid background of a wall or curtain with the light shining on them. Everyone knows how difficult it is to arrange flowers against the light. You cannot see properly what you are doing. The same applies when flowers are standing in a window; the colour contrasts and the whole group look somewhat confused. Flowers are most satisfactorily illuminated from above or by a spotlight positioned suitably. Only very occasionally is light from behind effective. This occurs with certain flowers with translucent petals, for example Poppies.

If you intend to use flowers to emphasise the wall colours, or a decorative object in the room, they should be set up near the chosen feature. This was well illustrated when we recently decorated one of the stately homes. We used red flowers and foliages in reds with some grey/greens, such as Eucalyptus, in a long trough on the mantelpiece under a magnificent painting – *The Resurrection* by Johann Rottenhammer in the 'Red Library'. The wall covering was in red and gold, with a superb ceiling in the Wedgwood style with gilt plaster and black oblong painted panels. The picture background was also in black, with its wonderful flower garland made up of posies of flowers in red, pink and white. The result was a wonderful, rich display, just right in this rather ornate setting.

Sometimes in a very 'busy' room it may seem impossible to get a clear area for flowers. Perhaps it is the wall covering that makes it difficult. This is no real problem because you can hang up a piece of a suitable plain material as you would hang a tapestry or a large map and then stand your flowers in front of it. An unwanted doorway can be disguised in this way. At the same time flowers can be used to stop people reaching prohibited places. I was once decorating a castle in Scotland. In a large, upstairs hallway there was a small spiral staircase in one corner, going up to one of the turrets which was deemed to be dangerous. To hang a curtain here would have looked somewhat incongruous, so instead an enormous mixed-green arrangement, make up with such things as Gunnera (giant Rhubarb), Angelica, Teasles and Onopordon Thistles was made up in a cattle trough. It looked fantastic and it served its purpose well. Nobody could have moved it or got past. The old, dull, galvanized finish of the trough worked in well with the grey stone wall.

A large mirror makes an interesting background for flowers if you remember certain points:
1)   The mirror will multiply the number of blooms required in the group, especially those at the back and sides.

A modern vase with cherry blossom and megasea leaves

This vase lends itself for use with simple branches of flowering Cherry or another blossom. The round, flat Megasea leaves take off the round shape of the vase. By using this type of material you get a happy association between flowers and the container.

It is important to get a good balance with your material when using a container like this, which is nearly round in shape. I find it makes sense to half-fill it with sand or gravel to make it really heavy and stable, and have a little 2" wire netting in the top half of the vase and choose stems which are not too heavy. A pointed end to the stem will help drive it into the sand or gravel.

2)   See that the back of the vase is clean, tidy and that no netting is showing.
3)   Get a good framework of foliage before adding any flowers and go right into the back of the vase. This acts as a foil and you then get a clearer outline and shape to the final vase.

One background that can be a problem should be noted. That is when you are arranging flowers in front of a picture. In my experience with the Constance Spry School, I have found that it always crops up when arranging flowers in one of the main rooms of The Guild Hall in the City of London. This room has at the one end a wonderful, stained-glass window set above a very narrow ledge which is quite high up. The ledge is an ideal place for flowers but narrow, so to get a tall group to rest there in a container that sits safely is a work of art. But it is at the other end of the room that the real problem arises. There are two superb marble fireplaces – one each side of an attractive doorway – and over these are mantelshelves which are wide enough to hold a good vase of flowers. Unfortunately over each fireplace are valuable oil paintings that are not protected in any way. When arranging flowers, you must see that no branches or stems protrude backwards that might scratch the surface in any way. In fact, you should keep everything low down and flowing over the front.

Drapes

The addition of a drape as background can make a very big difference to a display, whether it is behind a large group standing in a hall, or used as part of a setting where a number of items are displayed. It is important that it is of the right colour and texture to 'lift' the subject in front of it. It should not be overpowering or detract from the subject but rather enhance it and make the flowers stand out. It may be there to hide an undesirable object which cannot be moved, or to take away a background colour that is not correct, or it may be an addition to add interest and highlight the subject.

Drapes can make or mar a display and they must be used with care. They should always be in perfect condition, well ironed and correctly hung. There is a lot to be learnt about hanging material. Drapes are used a lot in the Far East when white walls can be covered very effectively in wonderful silk murals. In this country they need to be handled with great care, otherwise they can look out of place, and sometimes they attract rather than detract from the object they are supposed to be covering. Some of the modern hotels have alcoves backed with materials which are most attractive. The secret is getting the correct colour and lighting along with the ideal shape. A good material background is easier to use than a mirror as a backing. The mirror tends to show up any defects and, if the flowers are not carefully arranged, can make the vase appear overcrowded and perhaps untidy.

5. Arranging your flowers

Cutting and preparation

Before setting out to cut your flowers for decoration, have a picture in your mind of the arrangements which you wish to create. This will avoid wasting materials. It is easy to carry on cutting and then, at the end, to find you have twice as many flowers as are necessary for the job in hand.

If you are cutting from the garden, I suggest you do this in the early morning or late evening. Take a deep bucket of warm water in which to put the freshly-cut stems. Picking in the evening means the flowers can have a long drink overnight and be ready for use the next morning. Many people make the mistake of cutting in the hot part of the day and lay the flowers down to wilt as they pass from plant to plant.

Remember that some flowers are not so long-lasting as others, so to obtain the best results cut when they are just breaking bud and they will develop in water. The problem of whether to use a knife or scissors often crops up with gardeners – the old school always say use a knife, but this does not really worry me. Use whichever you find the easier but always make a clean cut, cutting back to a side shoot. A good pair of secateurs may be the answer because these will cut through any stem. Do not tug at the plant, and do not cut too hard. Always leave some growth above soil level to go on growing.

Carry a picture in your mind as you select your stems. Those with natural curves, so often discarded by the commercial grower, will help to give a free-flowing natural look to the finished vase. As soon as your picking session has finished, take your flowers and prepare them properly to prolong their life.

Increasing interest in flower arrangement has inevitably added to our knowledge of flower care. We know how we can help flowers last well when cut, and also how some flowers and leaves, once considered too short-lived to be worth cutting, can be made to last reasonably well. There are many different theories: some people always make their second cut under water to stop any air-lock forming, while others will only cut with a knife.

Have containers of fresh water ready to hold the prepared stems. If the flowers have travelled a long distance and are limp, you should put them into warm water. Remove anything superfluous, such as a damaged leaf, a broken side-shoot or foliage which will clearly come below the water line of the vase. A mass of leaves submerged in a vase not only takes up room and limits the amount of water but it also very soon makes the water discoloured and unpleasant; and with some materials, such as members of the cabbage family like Stocks and Wallflowers, it soon develops a nasty smell.

For convenience I divide flowers into groups. Consider first materials with hard, woody stems, including Larkspur Stock and perhaps older stems of plants like Wallflowers and Nicotiana. Remove the bottom leaves, cut the stem at an angle and then cut about half an inch up the tip of the remaining stem with a sharp knife, or hammer it to break the tissues thus allowing water to penetrate into the woody fibres. Some flower arrangers scrape off the outside bark or rind of the stem.

The next group, with soft fleshy stems, includes Hyacinth, Calendula and Arum. Cut the stems at an angle and place at once under water. Remove any unwanted foliage before cutting.

My third group contains flowers with stems that bleed. The Poppy family is a good example, as well as the Euphorbia in its many kinds. As soon as a cut is made through the stem, a white milky liquid appears. This should be stopped by plunging the tip into boiling water for a few seconds, or by placing it in a flame for the same period of time. If you use boiling water, protect the flower and any foliage from the steam. Poppies, by the way, should be cut just as the buds are breaking; then they will last quite well.

Sometimes a problem occurs with thick, hollow stems. It is not likely to be serious with annuals but plants such as Delphinium, Lupin, Hollyhock and large Dahlia come into this group. With a hollow-stemmed flower it is sometimes helpful to fill the stem with tepid water from the spout of a small can or teapot and then plug it with cotton-wool before placing it in deep water. This assists the capillary action, and I also find that it helps to stop Zinnias from bending over just below the flower head. In fact, Zinnias are the only flowers that I think should be wired before arranging in a vase and I do this by pushing a 22 gauge wire up to the head inside the hollow stem. You can, if you prefer, make a hook on the wire end, and push the point of the wire through the flower head down into the hollow stem until the hook is in the petals. Any flowers which appear to be flagging and unable to support their heads are the better for being wrapped up in stiff paper and given a long drink. This helps the stems to take up water, and, once fully charged, the flowers will develop in flowing lines. Certain flowers drink up a surprising amount of water during the first few hours after arranging. More flowers than is generally realised are lost through inadequate filling up of the container.

For an arranged group of any size, particularly of mixed flowers, the vase should initially be filled up to the brim. It should then be inspected after a few hours and again topped up, preferably with warm water. There is no need, provided the stems have been freed of foliage below the water line, to change the water at frequent intervals.

Most cut flowers cannot stand up to hot dry air. It soon robs them of their natural moisture and causes them to wilt and then, if not quickly treated, to die. They should be protected from the direct rays of hot sunshine. Keep arranged flowers away from direct heat from radiators and see that they are always filled up with water. A word of warning here about water siphoning from a fully-filled vase. This may be caused by a leaf or stem leaning at an angle over the rim of the container. The damage is all too often done before the water is noticed on a polished surface.

Draughts are another problem and can cause serious troubles, especially

Chinese base in bronze

Here, a black bowl is set in a frame to hold flowers.
The arrangement contains Alder, Clivia leaves and a little Eucalyptus foliage with a few
Fatsia Japonica leaves to fill in the vase centre.
Three Clivia, 2 different Tulips, (yellow/orange), Straw Hyacinth, one stem of Orchid
(Cymbidium), Spray Carnation, cream Freesia, Lachenalia (Cape Cowslip) make up the
flowers in this late-spring arrangement in warm orange/apricot/yellow colourings.

with tender materials brought in from the moist, warm air of the plant house. An occasional spray with a fine mist will help keep a moist atmosphere around the cut foliage, but this must be done with care and not to the extent of allowing water to drip off the leaves. Place a piece of cloth under the vase whilst spraying to stop the fine film of moisture reaching the surface on which the vase is standing. If using a wall vase for flowers make certain that the surface behind the flowers is not damaged by the spray.

I have difficulty in understanding why people use many of the mechanical aids which are made to support and display flowers. Quite frankly there is nothing to beat using natural, long stems – you will get a far better group which will sit comfortably in the vase and appear part of it. Some of the stands you find today, set with iron uprights and cones, or tubes at the top and holders for oasis at the base, make use of shorter materials but they have to be packed so closely to hide the mechanics that the arrangements immediately look heavy and unnatural.

Constance Spry always advocated simple, flowering lines – they cut down on the material needed, and allow every flower freedom to show itself off.

Vase contents

I would be a rich man if I had been given a pound every time I was asked the question, 'How do you know how many flowers you need for a certain vase?' Unfortunately, this is a question nobody can really answer because no two people would do a vase in exactly the same way. So much depends on the following factors:
1)   The size of the vase;
2)   The size of the flowers and the stem length;
3)   The available foliage.
To get a really dramatic and large arrangement you need a heavy, well-proportioned vase and then long-stemmed materials with a few very large blooms for the centre weight.

Without long-stemmed material, no matter how many flower tubes you have available, a pleasing group cannot be made. Short material set up in tubes gives a contrived effect with no flowing lines. One good stem will give better results than six smaller stems. There are certain flowers that lend themselves to large arrangements, such as Lilies, Rhododendrons and large Chrysanthemums, whereas the largest head of a Hyacinth does not really look correct unless used deep down at the centre of a large group. Try to remember your material growing and use it in that way.

It would be impossible to list any sound advice dealing with numbers of stems. I would suggest that you get some practical experience by first choosing a suitable vase, then getting a bucket of long and large foliage and a bucket of mixed flowers. Start by placing in the foliage, making it as large as possible. Then get your centre worked out, with a few big leaves. Then arrange your outline flowers, bringing in the colours and material often going towards the centre because they appear heavy. Use everything and see how you get on. If you have not enough to finish the vase, your outline was too big. If the vase is too full, you could have had a wider outline. Only by doing this type of practical work will you get the idea for a large or medium group. Proportion is important and in many arrangements the vase plays an important part. Three, five or seven stems normally will do the outline foliage, with large leaves at the centre, then three or five large centre flowers and five to seven tall stems of Lily, Alstroemeria or long Chrysanthemums. Once the main framework is set up, it is a matter of using shorter stems to fill in. Do remember not to overcrowd and get fussy-shaped arrangements. Remember the advice Constance Spry herself used to give us as students: 'if in doubt, leave out'. It really makes sense and leads to a much better result.

When trying to work out amounts, draw up a list. Try to picture the final results for which you are aiming. Draw a line diagram for the position of each item. Gradually it will come together. Some flowers, such as Lilies, can be in three, five or seven stems. Others, such as Pyrethrum, will be bought in bunches of 10, so 10, 15 or 20 may be necessary to fill a gap. The smaller the individual flower the more of them will be necessary to make their mark. Remember the different stem lengths so that you get that 'in and out' feel to the flowers. One large arrangement will make more impact than three or four small groups, so for party flowers think big. Something on a pedestal always stands out well.

Holding flowers in position

There are many people who know just what picture they want to create with their flowers but have no idea how to make the stems stay firmly in position. The old idea when staging flowers for a show was to fill the vase with stems of greenery. These were often privet, or something similar, and the pieces came only to the rim of the base. Then into this the stems of those flowers to be exhibited were stuck. This is totally against the principle we follow today because the first golden rule is, no foliage below the waterline.

I still believe that the most successful way of holding flowers is to use 2″ wire netting. It allows a firm hold, freedom to get really good, natural-flowing lines and a maximum volume of water in the vase. Some people find difficulty in handling wire and fear damaging their container when fixing it inside so they prefer using one of the foam substances. Some use the two together which gives the best of both worlds and makes sense, especially if the vase is to be moved around. I have to admit that just using a form of Oasis is the quickest way to get a firm anchorage and to that end it suits many decorators who are hard-pressed for time.

Whatever you use, remember that you are creating a picture with your vase and flowers. In no way should any form of holding device be seen unless, of course, it is decorative such as a piece of crystal or interesting shaped rock or stone through which the stems flow.

Ordinary wire netting mesh – 20 gauge, 2″ in diameter – is the best one to use. I find the plastic-covered sort impossible, and a finer mesh, when crumpled up, is too small to allow other than the thinnest stems to be threaded through it. The netting is first cut into a square or rectangle – the amount you

Gentians as a desk decoration

Arranged in a wonderful blue and gold oriental vase standing on a little matching tray, these striking gentians were just tucked into the small container together with some silver grey foliage.
There is nothing more beautiful than the gentian and it lasts well in water.

need to use for each vase will soon become apparent. By practising with a few containers you will arrive at the correct amount. All the wire has to do is support and hold the stems in position. The less there is in the vase, the better in some respects. Again, thicker stems will tend to need less netting, provided it is firmly held in the vase. The number of layers will depend on the depth of the vase but ideally there should be a layer on the base of the container and an area in a dome just above the vase rim to give good support to the tallest material, with two to four layers in between. Secure it by tying it in like a parcel. When arranged the tie should be cut away and, if it is a balanced arrangement, everything should stay in place. In fact, it may be left tied in because the string or wire should not show. Another quick method is to use rubber bands. Clip a few 'ears' of netting over the rim to stop any slipping. Whatever you do, always have your netting firm before starting any arrangement.

When using a glass vase – not easy because the stems show so clearly – just a small tangle of netting in the top should help to hold the stems, which must be clean and attractively placed. Oasis is out of the question in this type of container. A plastic or metal container of any shape may have a small piece of Oasis in the base with a little netting over the top. The oasis holds the first few stems and the rest tuck into them and hold firmly. Stems should all radiate from the centre of the vase and not cross over each other.

There have been all sorts of different types of netting used in conjunction with suction pads for instance. One is called a mazie, but it is most awkward to use and the netting is always of a fine mesh – only suitable for light stems and small arrangements.

OASIS   This cellulose sponge is expensive to buy and needs to be used properly. Never use more than you really need for any arrangement. Allow plenty of water reservoir around the block which should always be kept full. Many people fill the container with the Oasis and, once the flowers are placed in it, forget to top up with water and do not touch it until they notice the flowers looking tired, by which time it is often too late to revive them. Once dried out, oasis does not take up water so well again. There are different types of Oasis still being brought on to the market always with a view to holding more water and absorbing it more quickly.

For commercial work you do not have to worry about the length of time you can use Oasis because after each arrangement it is thrown away, but for the household purposes you want a substance that can be used a number of times before it disintegrates, as this keeps costs down. One that takes all types of stems and holds them equally well is the 'ideal' substance, useful because so often you use mixed stem types together. 'Springtime', brought out for soft stems, seems to be used less today. Students should watch the press for new lines coming out. Try them, it is always worth it, and make up your own mind what you use for the future.

PINHOLDERS   For certain types of arrangement, when using a shallow container, the pinholder is a useful form of flower holder. It originated in Japan, is made of a heavy metal base with sharp pin points standing up from it. In varying diameters and with pins of varying lengths and thickness, you

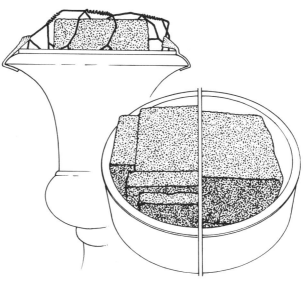

Oasis in containers. The container at the back shows the correct height for the oasis to stand above the vase rim, with a layer of netting held with Oasis tape. The flat bowl in front is incorrectly packed on the left hand side, with too much Oasis; the single piece on the right hand side is quite enough to hold the stems and allow plenty of water.

choose a size and type to suit the container and materials being used. Of more use for thick and fleshy stems, it can be used for thin stems by first impaling a small ball of netting through which you thread them.

Some pinholders are set in small shallow containers and these in turn are set in a larger shallow dish. This keeps a little reservoir of water in a small area but it must be filled up all the time. This is known as the 'well pinholder' or Kenzan.

I would like you to study the following detail:
1) Choose a block of Oasis and thoroughly soak it for 3–4 hours to get the whole block fully charged with water.
2) Select your container, clean it and place it on the table ready to use.
3) Assess the amount of Oasis needed to make a good stem-holding unit in the middle of the container.
4) Cut the block across to satisfy that requirement.
5) Do not trim off more Oasis than is really necessary. It should be just a little higher than the rim of the vase, fitting in easily with water space all round.
6) If you wish, place a piece of wire netting over the top and tuck it into the sides of the vase.
7) Secure with string, wire or Oasis tape, to the sides of the container to make everything firm.
8) Top up half way with water.
9) Do not use a pinholder in the base of the vase – it is useless and quite unnecessary.
10) The piece of Oasis not used should be kept damp and used as soon as possible. Do not let it dry out because it will not be so successful the next time you use it. Eventually, with practice, you will probably only cut enough to satisfy your needs for each vase.

A section through a bowl, showing a pinholder and wire netting held in position with tape

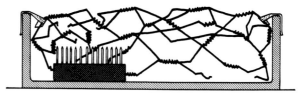

11)   If working with dried materials and Oasis 'Sec' then you can use a special 'frog' (a name given to a special type of pinholder used in conjunction with Oasis). It has a heavy metal base but only five or so, pins on which to impale it. Dry sand and gravel may also be filtered in around the brick to hold it firm and add weight. I also use a piece of netting over the top, which I secure to the vase rim, making everything extra firm.

There are two items which you will probably not find useful, but they often crop up when customers send their own vases to the shop to be filled. One is the wire cage – you have all seen them in the silver rose bowl. This makes every stem stand upright. The other is the glass dome, which is very heavy and ungainly, and only useful in the base of the container to make it balanced when using heavy stems. If you don't use them see that they· are carefully returned with the completed order.

Any expensive container should be lined with brown paper before wiring up. This will stop the surface becoming scratched. Arrange, then fill up with water.

Mixed garden flowers (opposite)

Mixed summer garden flowers in a white footed tazza: a real summer group I collected when walking round the garden. All were growing outside in the herbaceous border or the annual cutting bed. No set pattern is followed – just stems flowing from a centre point with much variation of stem length so that each flower head shows to good advantage. Small-leafed Eucalyptus, a little Elaeagnus and some Megasea leaves are the only foliage. The group fits well standing on a small table in the corner of the stair-well.

Eucalyptus	Alstroemeria (2)
Eleagnus bungii	Antirrhinum
Atriplex Nortensis rubra	Dahlia (mixed pom and small
Megasea	decorative)
Golden rod (Solidago)	Godetia
Kniphofia	Delphinium
Lupin	Molucella laevis
Foxglove	Rudbeckia
Galtonia Candicans (summer	Lilium
Hyacinth)	Euphorbia
Gladiolus	Cardoon
Larkspur	Sedum
Phlox	Statice
Stock	Salpiglossus
	Polygonum bistorta

Mixed garden flowers

LEAD STRIPS   There are occasions when one uses baking tins, for example, on church windowsills and these often are not large enough to hold a lot of water safely. The water is necessary to balance the arrangement. Strips of lead will be most useful in these cases. They take up little room and are very heavy. Cut them to fit the base of the container and you will find them excellent. A builder or roofing contractor may be able to give you a little that he has left over from a job.

Old lead, though expensive can be flattened and shaped to fit containers and it is clean and simple to use. Gravel and sand take up more space for the given weight and are messy to handle.

Flower tubes

The use of these tubes enables you to add a small amount of short-stemmed material to a large group, but they must be used with care and never in large numbers.

Many people have the wrong idea with tubes and believe that if they have a large number of them fixed to a stout stick in the vase they can build up a framework for a large group. This is not so. To get a really well-arranged, large group of flowers you need long-stemmed flowers and interesting branches of foliage which can make the framework to the arrangement. The tubes, hidden within the greenery, will hold and support the shorter flower stems which, if not lifted up, would be lost.

Tubes can be of metal or plastic, and usually come in a size of about 12″ in length and 1½–2″ across the top. They need to be about this size to allow a little netting to be placed in them, and it is also important that they hold enough water. You can, if you are so inclined, make your own tubes from washing-up liquid bottles, with the top cut off, fixed to a bamboo cane. They should be painted green to help camouflage them. I prefer them on square sticks which grip and hold more firmly in the wire netting than round ones. The sticks should vary in length so that you can make an arrangement of five to seven points in the vase – never use more than this if you want lovely, flowing lines to your group – before placing in the foliage. The tubes should radiate just as your stems do in the vase. White tubes are available but they show up and defeat the object of the exercise.

Always fill the tubes up with water before starting and make a mental note of where they are – a practical point when someone else is maintaining your group for you such as at flower festivals. Tell them, with a sketch, where the tubes are and how many there are. Provided your materials have the correct treatment in the beginning and that the water table is kept up, your flowers should last well. I prefer tubes in wire netting to Oasis, because I think they are safer.

Another point to remember is that the vase you use in conjunction with your tubes should be really heavy, so that weight in the top of the vase could not topple it over. We always avoid using tubes if we can. If you need them, use them with care and see that your stems flow in the correct lines from the centre of the vase.

6. Types and techniques

Types of wire

The quality of a true florist's work can be judged very simply by the standard of the wiring. It is a very important factor and can make or spoil any piece of floristry. Wiring is essential if the proper shape is to be kept, and if the flowers are to stand up. Keep wiring to the minimum and avoid what I term 'over wiring'. It shows lack of confidence straight away and makes for pieces of floristry that appear over-rigid. Wherever possible, the wiring should be hidden (internal) and the flowers and foliages should retain their natural appearance. Your flowers should look like a beautiful piece of jewellery.

At present the supply of wires is very haphazard and it is not easy to get the fine wires. It is therefore difficult for me to lay down laws as to what you should use. All I would suggest is that the finest wire that will do the job satisfactorily is the best. Remember that you are not staking a stem; you should be just wiring it down lightly to support it. Unless we are making frames or special Christmas decorations, in the School we seldom use a heavier wire than 20 swg (0.90mm), and the majority of our mounting wire is not heavier than 22 swg (0.71mm). For wiring down stems, we mostly use 22 or 24 swg (0.71 or 0.56mm). So often what would appear to be an attractive piece of work seen from a distance proves to be ruined by heavy wires.

Wire sizing, like so many other things, has been changed to meet the rules and regulations of the EEC. The identification of gauges now appears in millimetres, as opposed to swg.

OLD AND NEW WIRE SIZES			LENGTHS OF WIRES		
swg	mm		ins	mm	
18	1.25		3½	90	
19	1.00		5	130	
20	0.90	x	7	180	x
22	0.71	x	9	230	
24	0.56	x	10	260	x
26	0.46		12	310	x
28	0.38		14	360	x
30	0.32	x	18	460	
32	0.28	x			
34	0.24				
36	0.20	x			

Those wires I find we use most often in the School are marked with a cross. Never use longer wires than necessary, but remember the extra length for

An autumn pedestal arrangement

This group contains a wealth of coloured foliages and flowers. Dahlias make a very good decoration but are better picked from the garden rather than bought from a shop, as they do not pack and travel well. On the right-hand side there is some 'hop' vine trailing over the pedestal. Atriplex Hortensis rubra and paeony foliage make a big splash of colour.

bouquet work will make for movement in the tail. When worked on a short wire you get a tight stiff appearance.

The stub wires in 20 swg in 10″ and 7″ (0.90 × 260 or 180mm) are used for mounting and wiring down heavy flowers. Swg in 14″, 12″ and 10″ (0.71 × 360, 310 or 260mm) are used for wiring down medium flowers such as Roses and Scabious, and for mounting some bouquets. Wires of 24 swg in 10″ and 7″ (0.56 × 260 or 180mm) are used for wiring down smaller Roses and light flowers, and for mounting some foundation work. The other finer wires are used for wiring small pieces and binding. They are usually bought as silver wire. Some mossing is done with blue annealed wire.

May I encourage you to use a 'wire tidy' – it helps to keep your wires in good condition and is easy to work from. Wire today is like gold-dust – not only is it scarce but it is so costly to buy. It should never be left lying on your work bench or allowed to get wet. It will soon go rusty and then make dirty marks when used with ribbons. Covered wire is good for this purpose but again seldom available in the market. A sensible wire tidy has a tray in front to hold other necessities – scissors, reels of wire and string. You can get one made to suit your own needs. I have seen them made from used cans secured to a strip of metal as a base. These serve their purpose admirably.

Wiring techniques

Try to remember these points:
1) Always use the finest wire that will do the job.
2) What you want is flowers to be 'held' yet to have 'movement'.
3) Hide the wire as much as you can, always going into the stem from the back.
4) Never use an extra twist as you work; the flowers will tend to support each other and become firm without the extra twist.

BINDING This is used to hold the flowers and leaves into position when making bouquets, sprays, head-dresses, and buttonholes. Silver reel wire is used, usually 36 swg (0.20mm) for sprays, head-dresses and buttonholes and 30 swg (0.32mm) for bouquets.

DOUBLE LEG MOUNTS For wreath work and bouquets: Hold the flower in the left hand, the head of the flower being on the top of the hand. Place the stub wire vertically at the back of the stem approximately ¾″ (1.8cm) from the base of the stem. The part of the wire below the stem is 1″ (2.5cm) longer than the part above the stem.

Bend both ends of the wire down to form a hairpin, keeping the wires to the width of the stem.

Hold the hairpin stem very firmly with the finger and thumb of the left hand and with the right hand wind the longer lower wire around the upper shorter wire and stem two or three times. Always wind away from yourself. The two legs should now be of equal length.

For sprays and head-dresses: when making a double leg mount on smaller flowers such as for sprays and head-dresses, wire with 32 swg (0.28mm) or 30

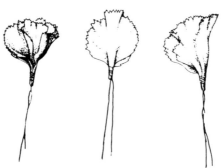

Feathered carnation petals

swg (0.32mm) silver reel wire, making the double leg mount in the same way as for the mounts on large flowers and foliage.

Sometimes when the flower is being mounted, the wire may be pushed through the flower or the stem before it is bent to form a hairpin, and then twist the wire round the stem three times.

EXTENDED LEGS   This is used when flower stems are too short and need to be made longer. The wired flower is mounted with a single leg mount with appropriate wire, the mount and wire then being covered with gutta percha. This is the term used when a wire replaces or extends a natural stem.

FALSE LEGS   This is the term used when a wire replaces or extends a natural stem.

FEATHERING   This is when separate petals are taken from a Carnation and wired together. Take one large petal, one medium and one small one. Have the large one at the bottom, then the medium and the small one on the top.

Make a pleat in the centre of these three petals holding them together. Push a 32 swg (0.28mm) silver wire through to hold the pleat in position and twist the wire three times round the Carnation petals. Bring the wires down as a single or double leg, depending on use.

Cut off the ends of the petals below where the twists of wire finish.

FOUNDATION WORK   Also called Based Work or Block Work. All flowers used are removed from their natural stems or left on very short stems. They are mounted or pinned to the frame in a flat mass. Cover the moss with tissue paper before pinning. This keeps the work clean. The smaller the flower the better the result will be.

GARLANDING   Ropes of flowers made for decorating pillars in a church or draped round tables at a wedding reception, etc. The flowers are wired with a single leg and the wire is twisted round three-ply string.

Take care that all the ends are on top of the string in order to prevent the scratching of furniture.

'GREENING'   In wreathwork the small pieces of green which have been wired together in threes with a double leg and the pieces placed into the moss on a frame, to cover the moss.

GROUPING   The term grouping is used when different flowers, foliage or a particular colour is gathered together to make a 'group' rather than have bits and pieces spotted about through the decoration. It applies in vases, funeral work and all make-up. Over-grouping can result in blocks of colour and can be too definite. It is better to have the colour, shape or what have you in 'sweeps' rather than blocks.

GUTTARING   This term is used for covering wires. Various materials are used and there are many different 'tapes' on the market. In the majority of cases gutta percha is used, this being obtained in green, white, brown and natural colours. It is a tape of rubbery texture which grips the wires and stretches slightly when gripped between the fingers. The warmth of the hand helps to soften it and, although not glued in any way, it does stick to itself.

   The secret of covering any wire is to get the material to lie flat on the wire and to run it down as quickly as possible. Always start on the stem of the flower where the mount begins and hold the material in the left hand between the thumb and first finger, with the wire beneath the thumb and first finger of the right hand. Place the gutta at an angle of 45° to the mount and start twisting the wire with the right hand, stretching the tape slightly with the left hand. Twist the covering down quickly to the base of the wire, and finish off by twisting it onto itself. Thin strips of silver paper can be used instead of the gutta but you cannot stretch them because they will break. Otherwise, the same method of covering is used – the narrower the strip the neater the cover.

LOOSE WORK   Used in funeral designs, the flowers stand away from the frame and each line around the frame is a different length. The in-between spaces are filled with foliage and the frame itself is lightly greened.

MOSSING   A term used in wreathwork. The moss is bound on to a funeral design with either string or wire.

PINNING FLOWERS   For wreathwork, when the heads of flowers are pinned to cover the moss on a funeral design. The pins are usually 22 swg × 3½″ (0.71mm × 90mm).

PINNING ROSES   Used to hold roses at the bud stage. Make a small hairpin about ½in (1.25cm) long, and pin the sepals against the petals. This keeps the petals from opening. Insert the pin through the chubbiest part of the bud.

PIPPING   Individual flowers are taken from the main stem of the flower, for example Hyacinth Bells from the stem of the Hyacinth. Use a double leg mount, usually 32 swg (0.28mm) and cover with gutta percha.

RETURN END   This term is used in funeral, bouquet, spray, head-dress and buttonhole work. It is composed of the flowers which are placed in after the centre of a bouquet has been reached. The flowers after the centre of a bouquet are placed in and face back to the top flowers.

Twin candles with centre candlecup

This candlestick has been chosen to hold the flowers on the table for a party with blue colourings predominating to pick up the room colour (curtains and table mats, even to the china with a blue band). This was set up to give an idea of the overall effect. Blue is not an easy colour and can well be lost in the evening light. Gayle Derrick has arranged the centre to each silver candlestick by using a special candle cup to hold a very delicate and charming arrangement and two pale blue candles fill the other holders. The whole thing has been done with small flowers and foliages which are lovely but time-consuming to do. The materials are:

Eryngium - small sea Holly	*Rue*
Delphinium	*Jasmine*
Heather	*Poppy seeds*
Calluna	*Anchusa*
Pulmonaria	*Nigella*
Symphoricarpus	*Salvia*
Cornflower	*Cecille Brunner Roses*
Hydrangea	*Garrya elliptica*

SINGLE LEG MOUNTS   Place the appropriate wire behind the natural stem. The upper wire should not be longer than the natural stem. Close the wires to form a hairpin and wind the lower wire two or three times around the upper wire and natural stem, the last twist being at the end of the stem. Straighten the long wire – this forms the single leg mount. The upper shorter wire must not extend past the base of the natural stem.

SPRAY OR CORSAGE   Flowers worn on the shoulder of a dress or coat are called either a spray or corsage.

SPRAYING UP   Spraying up is used in bouquet work when compound flowers and leaves are too heavy to place in as a whole. Take separate leaves or flowers from the main stem and wire the flowers with silver reel wire with a double leg. The leaves have a stitch and double leg of silver reel wire. The double leg of both the flowers and the leaves are covered with gutta percha from where the wire is twisted, to the bottom of the double leg which needs to be approximately 2½in (6.25cm) long.

When the flowers and leaves have been prepared in this way, they are then attached to a 22 swg × 14in wire (0.71 × 360mm). Always have the same type of leaf or flower and have three, five or seven leaves or flowers as a spray. It is better to have uneven numbers on the stub wire. Choose varying sized pieces; in the case of flowers begin with buds and work to larger flowers with leaves, small ones to larger ones.

Take the 22 swg × 14in wire (0.71 × 360mm) and the smallest flower or leaf and place its false leg against the stub wire so that it overlaps the top of the wire by 1in (2.5cm).

Bind with 36 swg (0.20mm) silver reel wire from the top of the stub wire down 1½in (3.75cm) of the false leg of the flower or leaf. Take the next-sized flower or leaf and place it to one side of the top one, letting the tip of it reach just beyond the base of the first flower or leaf. Binding the leaf or flower into position about an inch (2.5cm) away from the natural stem and with the same piece of binding wire, travel down with it to attach the false leg of this one to the stub wire.

Take the third flower or leaf to the opposite side to the second one and again an inch (2.5cm) away from the natural stem, bind to the stub wire. If more flowers or leaves are required, alternate them side to side, binding them to the 22 swg × 14in (0.71 × 360mm) wire. When the last piece has been placed in position, travel an extra inch (2.5cm) with the binding wire to hold firmly, before cutting the binding wire away.

Cover the stems with gutta percha by bending the pieces downwards, with the exception of the first one. Begin the gutta where the binding has begun at the top of the stub wire. When the gutta has travelled down to where the second flower has been bound into position, bend the flower or leaf back into its original position.

Gutta to the next flower in this way and then continue to the bottom of the 22 swg × 14in (0.71 × 360mm) wire. When gutta percha is used it is not always necessary to bind on with reel wire first, but use the gutta percha to bind and to cover the 22 swg × 14in (0.71 × 360mm) at the same time. In this case the pieces are not bent down but left in position all the time.

STITCHING LEAVES A term used when wiring leaves. The leaf needs to be supported for floristry. Take the leaf with a small stem attached and, keeping the back of the leaf uppermost, make a stitch three-quarters of the way up the leaf across the centre vein with silver reel wire, the gauge depending on the size and weight of the leaf. The stitch should be small so that it is hardly visible from the front.

Bend the two ends of the wire down to form a loop at the back of the leaf.

Have one of the ends of the wire coming down against the stem and twist the other wire round the wire against the stem of the leaf. If a double leg is required, leave the wire which goes down the stem fairly long. If a single leg is required, this should be no longer than the natural stem of the leaf.

When using large leaves for wreath work, such as Megasea, Hosta or Hedera canariensis, a 24 swg wire may be used as a support. The 24 swg (0.56mm) wire is hooked through the main vein on the reverse side of the leaf, the longer wire being brought down close to the main vein and wound around the stem.

STITCHING CARNATION LEAVES (TWO STITCHES)   Another method is adopted for thin pointed leaves, for example Carnation grasses.

Cut the bottom of the grass at an angle.

With a piece of silver reel wire, usually 32 swg (0.28mm) make a stitch in the grass approximately halfway up the leaf at the back and going at an angle across the centre vein.

With the same piece of wire, make a second stitch where the grass tapers before the point at the top, again at an angle across the centre vein and at the back of the leaf.

Bend over the tip of the wire so that it does not stand away from the grass. The piece of wire left at the bottom of the leaf is twisted round the part that has been cut at an angle.

STRINGING   A term used in wreathwork. String is twisted round to hold the moss onto a frame.

SWAGGING   Swagging has more shape to it than garlanding and is wider at the centre. Done on a mossed flat backed base, it is seen only from the front.

TEASING MOSS   When preparing moss to place on a frame, pull out the moss making it looser and remove any pieces of stick or foreign bodies.

WIRING DOWN   This is placing a wire into the head of the flower and wiring either on the inside or outside of the stem to give it support and to stop it from breaking. Various gauge wires are used depending on the thickness of stem and the weight of the flower.

Care must be taken that flowers are wired into the seed pods or else breakages may occur. The wire should not show through the flower head.

Zinnia in white vase

This attractive arrangement for the guest bedroom would be most welcoming. Rosemary Jeffcock has carefully chosen these pretty miniature Zinnia to go with the colourings in this decorative room at Winkfield. The small sprays of Ivy and Artemesia will dry well. All the Zinnias are useful but grow best in a warm, dry summer.

For a room with rather busy wallpaper (as here, seen in the side mirror on the dressing table), and highly-patterned cushions, something clean-cut and simple is all that is needed, and the white vase of three cherubs holding up a small bowl is ideal on this dressing table.

7. Flowers for wiring

lowers have to be wired very neatly, keeping the wire out of sight as much as possible. The wire is used to support the flower and should be just strong enough to do this, but not so thick as to make the finished work look heavy and rigid, a very common fault with many florists. The length varies as to how long you require the flower to be. Never bind over the foliage on the stem of the flower, but make sure the wire twists go between the leaves.

Hollow and soft-stemmed flowers have wires placed inside the stems but when the stem is hard, for example with Carnations, the wire has to be on the outside of the stem. Here it is essential to twist the wire round the stem, not the stem round the wire, keeping the wire close to the stem. Wire down quickly with not too many twists.

Great care must be taken so as not to damage the flower by bruising, because with soft stems, such as Tulips, this will cause discoloration which will quickly show up in the finished work.

I cannot attempt here to cover every flower; this would be quite impossible, bearing in mind the vast range available nowadays throughout the season. What I have endeavoured to do is to give a good cross-section of the different stems and textures and I hope you will be able to adapt the guidelines given for these to other flowers. There are no hard-and-fast rules, but the following are suggestions that we at the School have found to be effective.

ALSTROEMERIA Flowers with a compound head are wired with 22 swg (0.71mm) from the top of the main stem and twisted down the outside of the stem to the bottom. Each flower is wired down by placing a 32 swg (0.28mm) silver reel wire into the base of the seedbox and twisting quickly down the thin stem and once round the main stem. Each flower is treated in this way, making sure that the twists of each flower go in the same direction. The ends of the wires are cut short and tucked into the main stem.

ANEMONE A hollow-stemmed flower. A 22 (0.71mm) or 24 (0.56mm) swg wire can be used depending on the thickness of the stem. Holding the flower with the left hand and the wire with the right hand, push the wire up inside the stem. When the green collar of foliage is reached near the head of the flower, watch that the stem does not break, and carefully guide the wire through the solid piece here and then up into the head of the Anemone. Make sure that the wire does not come through the black centre. Many Anemones have a twisted stem, so gently bend them straight as the wire is pushed up.

ARUM LILY A soft-stemmed flower. If the flower is small a 22 swg (0.71mm) wire is heavy enough, but if it is large a 20 swg (0.90mm) is needed. Push the wire up inside the stem, from the bottom of the stem to the head. Make sure that the wire cannot be seen from the centre of the flower.

CAMELLIA As with Gardenias, the petals will bruise if touched by hand. Use cotton wool or cellular wadding. Remove the Camellia from the main stem and insert the two silver wires criss-crossed through the base of the flower. Place a cotton wool 'bud' at one end of a 22 swg × 14in (0.71 × 260mm) wire and place into position at the base of the flower in order to replace the natural stem. Secure in place by bending down the rose wires and twisting around the 22 swg (0.71mm) stub. Cover with gutta percha.

CARNATION A hard-stemmed flower, so the wire goes down the outside of the stem. Push a 22 swg (0.71mm) wire into the stem at the base of the calyx, making sure it goes in at the back of the flower. Twist once round under the head of the flower and then take the wire quickly down the stem, twisting as you go. Do not have too many twists.

CHRYSANTHEMUMS AND DAHLIAS These are hard-stemmed flowers. Generally a 22 swg (0.71mm) wire is heavy enough, but for exceptionally large Chrysanthemum blooms use a 20 swg (0.90mm). Push the wire into the inside of the stem approximately 3in (7.5cm) from the head, and push it up to the head. The bottom of the wire can then be twisted down the remainder of the stem on the outside. Buds of Dahlias and smaller flowers and buds of spray Chrysanthemums can be wired on 24 swg (0.56mm) wire which is taken down to join with the main stem and then cut away.

DAFFODIL This is a hollow-stemmed flower. Use 22 swg (0.71mm) wire. Hold the flower in the left hand and the wire in the right hand, and push the wire into the hole at the base of the stem and carefully up the stem. You will find a slight difficulty when you reach the dried-up papery tissue (spathe) because the stem of the flower is much thinner here and becomes more solid. With an even pressure, guide the flower carefully between the thumb and first finger of the left hand, with the flower resting on the top of the hand. The wire should just reach into the seedbox, and not, as often happens, come out into the Daffodil trumpet, where it will show.

EUCHARIS LILY This exquisite flower requires careful and delicate wiring. Remove from main stem. A hollow tube 'stem' now remains. Cover the tip of a 22 swg × 14″ (0.71 × 360mm) wire with a bud of dampened cotton wool. Insert the wire into the throat of the flower until the cotton bud is lodged snugly into the top of the tube 'stem'. The flower will be more securely wired if the seed pod is left intact; however, in order to obtain more depth for use the seed pod may be removed.

Pass a thin silver rose wire through the stem just below the petals. Bring both ends down and twist around the 22 swg (0.71mm) wire. Put gutta percha over the base of the flower and down the false stem.

Ivy in different forms:

A   *Five-spray of leaves*

B   *Three-spray of leaves*

C   *Back view of single wired leaf*

D   *Front view of single leaf, wired single mount*

E   *Wired natural spray*

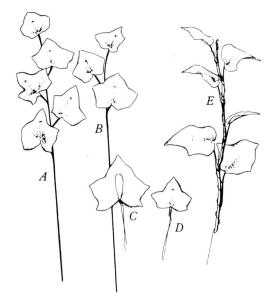

FOLIAGE   Large leaves are wired snugly, usually with a single stitch of reel wire at the top of the leaf and a large loop of wire at the back for support which is bound onto the base of the leaf stalk. For very wide leaves, two or three stub wires may be fanned out from the leaf base, ending in a small stitch on the leaf perimeter. The gauge of wire depends on the weight of the leaf.

Small fleshy leaves, are best used as growing tips; do not strip them down to the individual leaves. Wire with a fine silver reel into the growing point then down the stem, mounting onto a fine stub for use in a bouquet.

FREESIA   Freesia flowers need to be supported as well as the stems. This is done by taking a piece of 36 swg (0.20mm) silver reel wire and attaching it by twisting it on the main stem at the base of the bottom flower, twisting it on the main stem at the base of the bottom flower, twisting the wire up the flower to where it begins to bulge and then taking it down to the main stem. Thus giving the shape of a figure of eight.

When at the main stem, twist the wire up this stem to the next flower and wire it as for the first flower. Do this to all the open flowers but it is not necessary to wire the buds. Twist the wire up the main stem at the base of the buds until the top bud, then twist the wire round the base and cut the wire away. Take 30 swg (0.32mm) silver wire and push it into the stem where the 36 swg (0.20mm) binding wire began and twist down to the base of the stem.

GARDENIAS   The flowers of the Gardenia, whether used for spray or bouquet work, need to have a support of cardboard at the back of the petals. Never touch the petals of the Gardenia with your hand as their petals are so delicate they will immediately bruise and go brown. Move the petals with a piece of cotton wool or cellular wadding.

Take the Gardenias from the main branch. Cut a circle from a piece of cardboard and then cut a star shape in the centre of it.

Three leaves are required for backing the cardboard and they need to be the

Fruit and flowers on a flat dish

A flat, black, round dish makes an ideal container for this group of mauve, purple, lilac and pink flowers with black Grapes, Privet, Buck thorn, Sloe and Aubergine. Two different Chrysanthemums, Dahlia, Cobaea, Sedum and the last of the Roses with a late Antirrhinium. A touch of the second crop of Alchemilla adds a sharp green colour. The material is set in a small piece of Oasis at the back of the dish, the heavy fruit sitting well down in the bowl with the flowers built up around them.

same size and wired with 32 swg (0.28mm) silver single stitch, leaving a single leg with spike. Push the cardboard over the stem of the flower and up to the back of the petals to support them. Move the petals into position with the cellular wadding, to make a well-shaped flower. Break the calyx from the stem, push a 22 swg × 10in (0.71 × 260mm) wire through the stem under the cardboard and bend it down to make a hairpin with one long leg and one short leg; this should be level with the stem of the Gardenia. Push a 36 swg (0.20mm) silver wire through the stem and then place the three leaves round the cardboard, the short spike pushed into the stem, the single leg going straight down the side of the stem.

The leaves should show beyond the flower. Bind them on under their natural stems with 36 swg (0.20mm) silver wire and then down the stem of the Gardenia and a little way down the stub wire. Cover with gutta percha from where the binding wire begins down to the bottom of the stub wire.

GERBERA   For a bouquet, wire internally as far as possible. For long stems, go into the stem about 3–4in (7.5–10cm) below the flower and quickly twist the remaining wire down the outside of the stem. Do not come out through flower head. Use a 22 swg (0.71mm) wire.

GLADIOLI   The large flowers will need an 18 swg × 14in (1.25 × 360mm) for wiring down the stem. Place the wire into the stem just below the first flower and twist rapidly down the stem.

Bridal Gladioli should be wired on 22 swg (0.71mm) or 20 swg (0.90mm) up the stem and a silver wire from the first flower to the tip. Individual flowers are wired on double leg 32 swg (0.28mm) or 30 swg (0.32mm) silver reel – or if heavy, a single or double leg 24 swg (0.56mm) or 26 swg (0.46mm) wire.

HYACINTH   This is a soft-stemmed flower. Hold the flower with the left hand and the wire with the right, and push a 22 swg (0.71mm) wire up inside the stem until the top bell is reached. If the flower is extra heavy a 20 swg (0.90mm) wire can be used.

Hyacinth – spraying up bells:

A   *Single bell or pip*

B   *Three-spray*

C   *Five-spray*

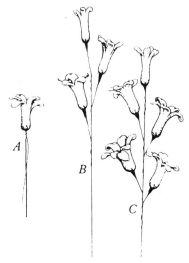

LILIES Push a 22 swg (0.71mm) gauge wire into the stem a few inches from the head of the flower and twist the wire down to the bottom of the stem. If there is more than one flower on a stem, wire the longest flower right the way down the main stem. Then wire the side flower to where the stem joins the main stem; twist round once on the main stem to hold it firmly in place.

LILY OF THE VALLEY This is wired from the base of the stem with 36 swg (0.20mm) silver reel wire, twisting very neatly up the stem between the bells and finishing with a twist round the base of the top bell. This needs great care as the wire can easily cut off the top bell.

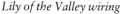

Lily of the Valley wiring

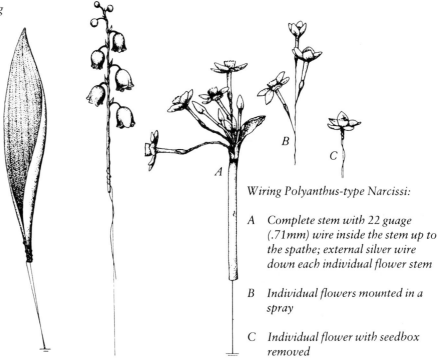

Wiring Polyanthus-type Narcissi:

A   *Complete stem with 22 guage (.71mm) wire inside the stem up to the spathe; external silver wire down each individual flower stem*

B   *Individual flowers mounted in a spray*

C   *Individual flower with seedbox removed*

NARCISSI When a Narcissus has more than one head on a stem, it needs to have a 22 swg (0.71mm) gauge wire inside the stem until the spathe is reached and then a 32 swg (0.28mm) silver wire pushed into the seedbox of the individual flowers and twisted down the stem to where the small stems reach the main stem. Then twist the wire round the main stem, cut it away and push the end into the main stem for a neat finish. All the wire from the small stems must be twisted in the same direction. If the individual flowers are fairly heavy, a 30 swg (0.32mm) wire can be used. It is not necessary to wire all the buds.

The spathe is removed for bouquet work, but it is not necessary to remove it for wreathwork.

For some varieties of Narcissi such as 'Cheerfulness', the 22 swg (0.71mm) wire can go beyond the spathe up into the stem of one of the compound flowers and the rest is wired with silver wire down to the main stem.

Flat posy of flower heads

This is not a new idea but it is seldom seen used. It dates back into early Victorian times and may be made up with many different flowers and foliages.

I have used a flat plastic Oasis base without the pad of Oasis. Instead I filled it with damp sand. You may wish to have an edge of greenery or prefer to work with an edging of lace. A sandwich cake tin will make an excellent container instead of the Oasis tray.

In this case I have used Portuguese Laurel cut to a set size and pinned carefully, each leaf overlapping to help hold firmly. Next I feel it important to set the centre point – a Rose makes the ideal flower standing out well. Now work your circles of flowers – just the heads on short stems which are stuck into the moist sand. You may use any flowers – not too large and of a similar round even shape. Bits of foliage may be worked in like Parsley, Ivy and Rue. Also small buds may stand up amongst the flowers. Keep to round rings. Add little bows to give a little relief.

It is surprising how well these arrangements will last if the sand is really moist and they are sprayed overhead from time to time. This arrangement will make good use of short stemmed flowers.

NIGELLA   These stems are often wiry. Pierce into the hollow part with a 22 swg (0.71mm) stub and secure the thin area with silver reel, going up into the flower head first and working down the stem to the heavier stub wire.

ORCHIDS   When using for bouquets and sprays, cut the orchid, leaving about ¾in (1.8cm) of stem. Wire up inside the stem with a 22 swg (0.71mm) or 24 swg (0.56mm) wire, length depending whether it is for a bouquet or spray. The wire needs to be 14in (35cm) long for a bouquet and 7–10in (18–25cm) long for a spray. Push a 32 swg (0.28mm) silver reel wire through the stem and twist down the stub wire a little way. Cover with gutta percha from where the binding wire is twisted to the bottom of the stem.

RANUNCULUS   Often these are hollow stems, but they do have difficult joints where the leaves are attached. Try to wire internally going up into the flower head. The heavy flowers often bend over at the neck and need support. Use 22 swg (0.71mm) or 24 swg (0.56mm).

ROSES   Roses are hard-stemmed flowers, so the wire needs to go on the outside of the stem. The gauge used depends on the size of the flower, either a 22 swg (0.71mm) or 24 swg (0.56mm), and also whether it is for wreathwork or bouquets. If the rose is in a bride's handspray a thick silver stub wire is used. Push the stub wire into the base of the seedbox at the back of the flower, close to the stem and twist it round once near to the head, then continue twisting the wire down to the bottom of the stem. Take the twists down quickly and do not have them close together.

SCABIOUS   Where possible, wire internally, but often, after the first pair of leaves down the stem from the flower head, the stem becomes thick and the wire may well then have to be external.
   Go well into the flower head but make sure that the wire does not show. Use a 22 swg (0.71mm) wire, 10–14in (25–35cm) in length.

Rose sprays:

A   *Single wired leaf*

B   *Individual rose mounted*

C   *Three-spray of rose leaves*

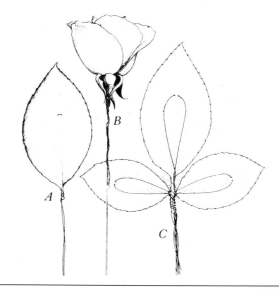

SNOWDROPS Wire them as for Violets (see below) but push the wire into the base of the seedbox and quickly twist down the outside of the stem. If the stem is very weak, bind in the little paper sheath to give it extra support.

STOCK OR LARKSPUR These have small flowers up the stem. You will have difficulty in trying to wire to the top of the stem, so use the following method. With Larkspur push a 22 swg (0.71mm) wire up the centre flower stem, and with Stock push the wire into the inside of the stem, a few inches from the top and then twist down the outside to the bottom of the stem. In both cases go as near the top as possible, then finish off the tip with 32 swg (0.28mm) silver reel wire to connect with the 22 swg (0.71mm) stub wire. Pierce the 32 swg (0.28mm) wire into the base of the first flower or bud.

TULIPS A soft-stemmed flower, it is difficult to push a wire inside the stem of a Tulip when a long stem is required. So, push the wire inside the stem just below the first leaf on the stem, and then up the stem to the head. Twist the bottom part of the wire round the outside of the stem below the first leaf and down to the bottom of the stem.

VIOLETS These are wired usually with 36 swg (0.20mm) silver reel wire. Push the wire into the top of the head, bend it round the stem and twist the wire down the remainder of the stem. Do see that the wire follows the contour of the Violet 'neck'.

WATER LILY These make wonderful flowers for a special summer table setting. They do not travel well so should be obtained locally and treated straightaway.

The flowers close once the light fails so to keep them open, carefully wax the base of the petals; then they cannot close. This is done by placing a few drops of warm (not too hot because it damages the petals) wax, but it must be warm enough to run through the base of the petals before setting.

Wire the thick, fleshy stems for make-up with a 22 swg (0.71mm) or 20 swg (0.90mm) wire internally.

Wiring of flowers for head-dresses, sprays and for 'spraying up'

Flowers may be used whole or, if too large, in smaller sections when making a spray or head-dress, but it is important that these are not too small. One reason is that they do not last so well and another is that the effect is lost and the spray or head-dress looks over-wired and bitty.

With most flowers the wire is pushed through the flower just above its base and the wire is twisted two or three times round the stem to form either a single or double leg mount. Some very small flowers are 'clumped' together and then mounted and some need to be wired up the stem first and then mounted.

The following list describes the wiring of various flowers. If a certain flower is not described then wire as for a flower of similar shape.

ALSTROEMERIA   Take a single flower from the main stem, leaving a small stem on it. Push a 32 swg (0.28mm) or 30 swg (0.32mm) silver wire, if the flower is heavy, through the base of the flower and mount it.

BLUEBELLS   Some of the flowers are wired singly with 32 swg (0.28mm) silver wire through the base of the flower and then mounted.
    The buds can be wired in a clump, especially the tip end of the Bluebell, with 32 swg (0.28mm) silver wire pushed through and then mounted.

CHINCHERINCHEE   Some flowers are wired singly with 32 swg (0.28mm) silver wire through the base of the flower and then mounted.
    The buds can be wired in a clump, especially the tip end of Chincherinchee, with 32 swg (0.28mm) silver wire pushed through the buds and then mounted.

ECHEVERIA   These are usually wired in clumps with 32 swg (0.28mm) silver wire pushed through the flowers and then mounted.
    They can also be wired singly with 32 swg (0.28mm) wire through the base of the flower and then mounted.

FORGET-ME-NOTS (MYOSOTIS)   Wired in clumps, these are tightly bound together with 32 swg (0.28mm) silver wire which is then taken down the stems to form a mount.

Cincherinchee:

A   *Individual flower wired*

B   *Individual flower wired and covered in gutta percha*

C   *Five buds and flowers sprayed up*

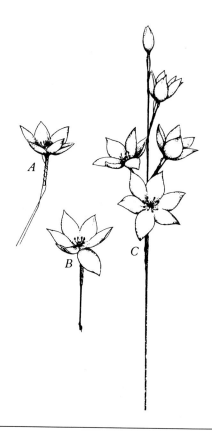

Late spring flowers on a flat dish

Japonica (Chaenomeles lagenaria)	Mini Daffodils
Hyacinth – secondary flowers	Hellebores
Heather	White Muscari
White Bride Anemone	Blue Muscari
Fritillaria	Primroses
Arum Italicum	Anemone Blanda
Osteospernum	Euphorbia robbaeii
Marguerite	Helleborus orientalis
Fennel	Alyssum
Osmanthus	Geranium Crispum – green and variegated
Iris	Chionodoxa
Golden Philadelphus	Forget-me-not

FREESIA   These can be wired as single flowers with 32 swg (0.28mm) silver wire and then mounted. Sometimes they are left at their full size or they may need to be cut shorter.

When shorter flowers are needed, cut them off above the stem and gather them together at the base. Wire with 32 swg (0.28mm) silver and mount.

Freesia buds have a 36 swg (0.20mm) wire twisted up the main stem between the buds on a spray, beginning at the larger buds at the bottom and working to the smaller buds at the top. To finish, twist the wire round just beneath the smallest bud and cut the wire away.

Mount with 32 swg (0.28mm) silver wire.

GENTIANS   32 swg (0.28mm) or 30 swg (0.32mm) silver wire is used depending on the weight of the Gentian. The wire is pushed through the base of the flower and then mounted.

HYACINTH   32 swg (0.28mm) or 30 swg (0.32mm) silver wire is used depending on the weight of the flower. The wire is pushed through half way up the bulge on the bell of the Hyacinth.

HYDRANGEA   Use two or three florets together keeping the flowers fairly level at the top. With 32 swg (0.28mm) silver wire have one piece of wire going straight down the stem, and twist the other piece of wire immediately beneath the florets and then three times round the stems.

Hydrangea florets:

A   single leg mount for a head-dress

B   Double leg mount for spraying up

C   For use in foundation work

LILY OF THE VALLEY   This usually needs to be cut in half and the two pieces used separately.

Each piece is then wired from the base and the wire twisted up between the bells on the main stem finishing with a twist round the base of the top bell. This needs great care as the wire can easily cut off the bell. Each piece of Lily of the Valley is then mounted with 32 swg (0.28mm) silver wire. Two pieces of Valley can be mounted together or a piece of Valley and a leaf can be mounted together if required.

MIMOSA   If the flowers are close together on the stem, they can be clumped together and bound tightly with a 32 swg (0.28mm) wire. Then make a mount.

If the flowers are more spread out, twist a 36 swg (0.20mm) wire up the main stem, and then mount with 32 swg (0.28mm) silver wire.

NIGELLA (LOVE IN A MIST)   Push a 32 swg (0.28mm) silver wire through the base of the flower and mount it.

'PAPER WHITE' NARCISSUS   The Narcissi are best left with the seedbox on, but when they are going to be cut very short to give depth to the spray or head-dress they need to be cut just above the seed pod. The 32 swg (0.28mm) silver wire should be pushed through the seed pod, so that the flower is left natural, and then mounted.
   When the seedbox has been removed the 32 swg (0.28mm) wire is pushed through the flower a little way up from where it has been cut.

ROCK CYCLAMEN   Push a 32 swg (0.28mm) silver wire through the base of the flower and mount it.

SNOWDROP   Push a 32 swg (0.28mm) silver wire through the seedbox and mount it.

STEPHANOTIS   These are usually left with a small piece of stem, but are sometimes cut above the base of the flower to give shorter flowers. This is to give depth to sprays and head-dresses. Push 32 swg (0.28mm) silver wire through the base of the flower and mount.

STOCKS   If the flowers are large take a 32 swg (0.28mm) silver wire and twist it round close to the petals to hold them into position.

Stephanotis:

A   *Individual flower mounted*

B   *Five pips sprayed up*

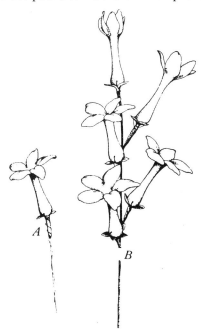

A Royal bouquet

Although most bouquets for special occasions require wiring (see Chapter 11), Royal bouquets should never be wired as they are later untied to be displayed in a vase. This is just a simple tied bunch which was prepared for the Queen Mother on the occasion of the Domesday Service in Westminster Abbey in 1986. It is easy to hold, light to carry and neutral in colouring so that it can be held against any colour scheme. In this bunch, we can see white roses, cream baby orchids, white freesia and lovely variegated foliage, all tied off with a good ribbon bow.

8. *Dried flowers*

*Y*ou often hear these mentioned but what, in fact, are they? If you look in any flower shop window that sells other than just cut flowers and plants, you will see arrangements of 'dried flowers'. On closer inspection these will include seed heads in various forms, cones from different conifers wired on false stems, maybe some pressed or glycerined foliage and, quite often, man-made flowers. These flowers can be made up of different parts of real plant material glued together to make different shaped flowers and then secured to false stems. One of my old students had a very successful business making these flowers in Kenya when I was out there a few years ago and, in their natural colouring, they made excellent shapes to add to a flower group. She was exporting them to many countries. Really the term 'dried flowers' covers all forms of plant-life which has been preserved in some form to use in long-lasting arrangements.

Today, combining silks with dried materials can make very interesting decorations. The main point to remember is getting the correct colour combinations and, as far as possible, using natural, not dyed, materials. In certain instances, even dyed materials, if very well done, may be incorporated in to the collection; however this immediately makes any arrangement look artificial. You may feel that, as a shop owner or assistant, it is not necessary to know about dried flowers but any background knowledge adds interest for your customer and could encourage sales.

Dried materials can be very attractive when well used, and you should always keep a look out for the good ones because they add an important aspect to your business. They are not something you want to store for long periods because they must be kept dry. Most fresh flowers need a moist atmosphere to keep well so they oppose each other in every way. One tip worth knowing is if they become too dry and brittle, place them in the cold store for 6–10 hours and they will soften slightly.

The main period for using dried materials is in the autumn when the outside crops become few, through to the Christmas decorations. They are used in a smaller way in the early spring, backed up with pots of the early bulbs and the first of the outside flowers and foliage. They should then be put away and, often, many should be thrown away. This is good for the flower trade because you have to start fresh again in the autumn! Having said that, I am the worst squirrel there is and tend to hold on to everything, as that odd box of bits is always useful!

If you are collecting dried flowers, there is never a period when you do not stand a chance of finding things. Start in the autumn, the peak period, and work through. When out walking in the winter, the bareness of leafy branches makes those seed pods and stems shown up so much better and also the lovely lines of licheny branches – if you are in an area of pure air and moist conditions – are so much more easily spotted. Watch for everything as it matures – material left on the plant provided the weather is kind is so much better. Muscari pods and Anemone pulsatilla seed heads really dry best outside – the latter when really fluffy need a fine spray of lacquer to hold them.

Only by growing things yourself will you get a wide range of shapes and colours. If you are a real gardener you will need two growing areas: one where you allow plants to flower and set seed naturally; the other where you encourage the plant to go on flowering by removing the seed heads all the time.

Some will say it is not necessary to have a garden to collect dried materials. To be fair this is correct but it certainly does help to widen the range. The hedgerow, field, lake-side and railway bank, to say nothing of that waste piece of ground in the town; all will have their own types of materials which will dry naturally on the plant or may be collected dried and prepared for keeping, such plants as Reedmace again needing a spray of lacquer to hold them intact.

There are many ways of collecting materials together to make a dried group and you must work on all avenues to get as wide a range as possible. Nature provides the greatest range from which to choose, but the timing for collection is the most important factor. The colours of the seed pods and stems change all the time and this is the detail which you must watch. Seed heads and berries will be there today and gone tomorrow, should the climate conditions suddenly alter. When collecting any material that is in short supply, let the seeds disperse first – really rare specimens should in no way be touched because sometimes that dried material above ground is protecting the root stock below from the winter conditions and if removed, you may upset nature and the plant may die.

Firstly I would suggest you look at the hedgerow and open country. Many fields today are harvested by large machinery which cannot necessarily follow all the contours of the field and boundaries. Consequently they do not reach the odd corners of the crop where there will be a wealth of material for the collector.

Ask before you attempt to glean, but most farmers will be only too happy to let you carefully cut some stems of such things as Oats, Wheat, Barley and Rye. All provide excellent material which dries so well and gives interesting shapes and texture. Many weeds run to seed and a wide range of seed heads will almost dry naturally on the plant.

Climbing plants in the hedgerows, such as the wild Clematis, make very attractive material in their final stages of development. Foxgloves and Teasel seed heads are quite excellent and Dock, although not wanted in the garden, if carefully collected and not shattered carelessly when clearing away, is another wonderful seed head. The Reed Mace must be collected at the right time but this is a useful tall subject for the back of a large group. I think it would be true to say that there is hardly ever a time when walking in the countryside or making a visit to a garden when something doesn't catch my eye and is collectable (provided this is allowed).

It may seem strange to say it but you do not necessarily have to have a garden to be able to do dried flower arrangements. If you have a railway bank close to home, a river or canal where plants may be growing at the water's edge, and the chance to get out in the countryside from time to time, all will be well.

The local florist, or even street market, will supplement your stock enabling you to purchase such things as Larkspur, Nigella and Statice in one or two forms, and Helichrysum. The more adventurous florist will sell fresh, South African wild flowers which also dry well. So it is just a matter of looking around and purchasing when you see the right thing. Achillea and Hydrangea are two other flowers you may see in shops. Your materials should be fresh and in good order when starting to dry them.

Having collected different materials you must prepare them for drying. This is important – a little time spent now will be well rewarded later on. Collect all the year round – the seasons will vary from year to year so keep your eyes open all the time. Once 'hooked' you will become very much more observant and in no time at all you will not miss a thing! That curved, bare branch, that lovely-shaped, Lichen-covered bark or may be just a perfect seed head of Gladioli – nothing will be safe!

The herbaceous border in the autumn holds a wealth of material and so much of it is dried by nature. I am always torn between two factors: whether to leave the seed heads for the birds or to collect them for my winter decorations. If there is enough to suit both needs, that is a happy solution.

In your garden try to grow special beds for your cutting material – these being allowed to run to seed in the latter part of the season. If seeds are produced early in the growing period, the flowering will tend to cease because the plant will have fulfilled its object in life. Always cut with as long a stem as possible. Clean up any unwanted material – broken pieces and foliage – so that only the best stems are used for drying. Any small pieces, interesting pods or short-stemmed flowers should be kept and dried on a wire netting rack. Always collect when the material is as dry as possible. Remove any unwanted bits and then hang up.

Methods of preserving

These fall into a number of different categories. The busy florist may not wish to be bothered with all these but it is a great saving if, when stock is not moving in its fresh form it is turned into a useful item for later on. Many times, materials are thrown away when – had the matter been given some thought – they could have been used in another way.

AIR DRYING This is an excellent way to dry your materials. It is nature's way, and nothing can be better than that. Just think back to your growing crops and remember those perfect seed heads of Lilies and Poppies, or those stems of papery flowers to be found in the border. It takes time to dry well but many flowers can be treated this way. Most of the material is dried by hanging upside-down and a golden rule is to remove all unwanted foliage. Remember the foliage always shrivels in the drying process and is not pretty in the long run so removing it carefully first saves time with the drying.

Always keep your materials in a dark area, free from dust and dirt. The old boiler house with the coke boiler was useless but today a sealed heating unit is clean and warm. If dried too quickly the flowers, in some cases, tend to shrivel up and become brittle so a warm atmosphere is ideal. Flowers develop after

A pewter container of dried flowers

A mixed arrangement of flowers which have all been air-dried except for the four pieces of Eucalyptus. These were first placed in glycerine and then allowed to dry once it had become darker showing that the moisture had been taken up. This allows the foliage to remain a little softer and less brittle.

The stems are simply arranged in a pewter pint tankard, in a piece of Oasis with some netting over the top.

The centre front has some pieces of Hydrangea well down and a piece of Hop on the left-hand side. You can see Wheat, Larkspur, Lavender, Rye, Helichrysum, Nigella seed pods, Polyanthus seed pods, Eryngium, various grasses, Echinops, Allium, Astrantia, Achillea, Statice and Gnaphalium.

they are picked and can change quite dramatically. Helichrysum must be only half open when cut, otherwise the flowers become open with flat, ugly centres. The time factor will depend entirely on the type of flower – those that are of a papery nature will be much quicker than those with thick, fleshy petals. Always tie up in small bunches held with a rubber band, or a slip knot, so that as the stems become thinner, they will not slip down and fall to the ground.

By keeping in the dark the flowers will keep a better colour. They do fade slightly but in doing so, take on a soft charm of their own.

Keep your different varieties together and, as soon as they are dried, store carefully in a dust-free area laid flat, and boxed up in old flower boxes with a little drying agent added to take up any moisture if the store is slightly damp. Watch from time to time to see that they are keeping well. Mice can be a nuisance with certain seed heads.

One well-known dried plant is the Chinese Lantern (Physalis). The swollen orange/yellow calyx is rather like a lantern and dries well holding its colour. Pick at the correct stage, having protected them from slug damage, and hang up by the top lantern so that they dry out with the lanterns hanging down. Removal of all leaves and any signs of late flowers is important.

Some dried flowers may be better if cut from the plant stems and wired whilst fresh rather than when in the dried state. Choose the flowers that are well developed but not fully out. I have in mind Helichrysum and that type of straw flower which tends to bend over when dried on the natural stem when it becomes very thin and brittle. Cut with about 1″ of stem, and wire this internally coming up into the flowerhead but not protruding through so that the wire can be seen. Sometimes people will thread this wire through a stem of straw once the flower has dried. The other way of disguising the wire is to bind it with gutta percha tape or something similar. Stems of dried flowers are always more prominent when arranged because there are no leaves left on the stem to hide them. The addition of a little silk foliage, which is extremely

Wiring helichrysum: left, wire up through stem so that wire just reaches the centre disk of flower; right, loop wire through head and pull wire down until the hook is hardly showing

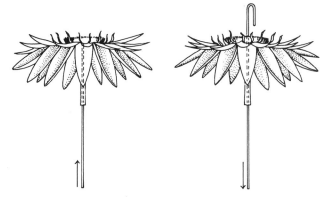

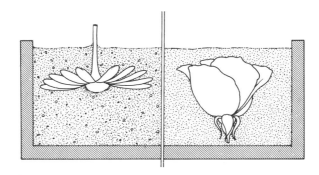

Drying flowers in sand: Left, daisy (head down); right, rose (head up)

realistic, will help with this matter. The flower arrangers doing the demonstrations for the day courses at Winkfield Place have occasionally added a piece of something artificial to a fresh or dried group and it has been interesting to note the audience reaction – some are shocked and others find it a wonderful idea. I am quite easy about it. I don't like gimmicks, but if you are using dried flowers and have the right colour and texture to do the job with pleasing results, I would be happy to support the idea.

WATER DRYING   This always seems strange to me but it really does work. I have used it successfully with flowers from abroad such as the South African wild flowers including Protea, Leucodendron and Heathers, and it is an excellent way of drying Hydrangea.

Put the freshly-cut stems into warm water – I suggest about 2″ and allow this to evaporate gradually without any topping up. You will find at the end that your flowers have dried slowly with very little change. When Hydrangea are dried by hanging upside-down, the petals tend to curl more.

DRYING IN A MICROWAVE OVEN   This is a very quick process and ideal for small quantities or very special flowers. You will need special microwave containers and lots of silica gel or similar drying agents.

The individual flowers need to rest on a bed of the drying agent, about 2″ deep, and to be covered very carefully with more of the powder getting it well into all the bases of the petals. The time taken is from 2–4 minutes at high power (using a 650-watt microwave). Remember that you must have a small container of water in the oven at the time.

SILICA GEL   This is an excellent, but expensive, way to dry flowers and one that should be used very carefully. It works quickly and well if you follow certain rules. Always have your drying agent in a fine powder form and in its bright blue colour. It changes with the moisture content, going quite pink when charged with moisture.

Dry it out in a slow oven and get it back to a deep blue before re-starting the procedure. It makes sense only to dry flower heads and to do this I make use of old plastic ice cream tubs. You may lay flowers down with the heads facing uppermost. Some people like to wire the flowers on false stems first when the wires must remain uppermost. Of course, when using flowers on false (wire) stems you cannot place them in the microwave. The wiring of some flower heads is so much easier before they are dried. I have in mind the Helichrysum, but in this case quite frankly it is such an easy flower to dry that one would certainly not waste time putting it in the microwave. The wired stem is covered with a green or natural flower tape or, in some instances, it is a good idea to thread it through a thin hollow stem or a straw.

Flower shops should consider holding stocks of a drying agent because it will be something that you can always sell. People are always asking for it and many chemists only stock the high-quality grade which is too expensive to use with flowers.

SAND   I am quite happy with a high-grade, clean silver sand – always keep some ready to use. Again, if you can stand a container on the storage heater, so that it remains dry, you will be ready to start the moment you get any flowers. One very important thing to remember is that your flowers should be really dry before you start – free from rain for at least 24 hours and picked in the early afternoon.

Silver sand is very heavy, so handle it with care. Lay your flowers flat on the bed of sand and from a small sieve lightly sprinkle a fine covering on to the petals. It should be worked right into the folds of each petal. Mark the area of each flower and carefully watch the development of the drying petal. It is good to keep each box separate and only work on one flower in each because you tend to damage the flower when you move it before it is properly dry. Date each box and record the time it takes to dry for future reference. Once you get into a routine, you can start to build up a stock of flowers then, when the time permits, you may work them into wall swags, pictures or other decorative pieces for sale. I always keep my dried material flat in air-tight boxes. Another idea is to stand them on a sheet of Oasis and keep them under cover.

The use of alum and borax helps with drying and some people recommend a dusting of either on to the petals when drying. It is very light, and maybe sprinkled onto the flower surface like icing sugar on a cake. On to this goes the dry silver sand. When dry, the whole falls away from the plant surface.

Another method is to start with a mixture of one part borax to three parts sand. A very fine paintbrush may be used to lift any trace of the white powder, should it appear to stick on the petals. Beware of those canisters of compressed air – they are excellent in theory but too strong in many cases and you may be left with just a collection of petals and a bare stalk. On really strong flowers they are excellent and they lift every particle of sand and powder.

Storage of all dried material is very important. It must never be allowed to become damp because this is when the grey mould fungus will set in. Store bunches flat or by hanging. Individual flowers in boxes or trays layered with tissue paper between and the odd sachet of silica gel helps to keep moisture at bay. A warm area is good. Watch out for mice when seed heads are involved.

PRESERVING WITH GLYCERINE   This is another way of building up long-lasting material for decorating. It is used mostly with foliages and those with fairly soft leaves are the easiest to do.

It does cause the colour of the material to change a little but it is very useful to have preserved foliage with which to work. Remember, no dried flower retains its foliage so you are always trying to hide bare leaves. Another useful item is stripped Lime and Hornbeam – the bracts are very decorative and retain a softness when preserved rather than being dried. Eucalyptus is another foliage worth treating. Select your pieces, prune out any unwanted branches, and then hammer the base of the stem for about 1″. Keep any small side-shoots because these may be treated and will be useful. For rather thick foliage use an equal amount of glycerine and warm water. For lighter foliage 1/3 glycerine to 2/3 water will be strong enough.

Use narrow buckets, or cylinder-type containers, allowing about 6″ of solution in the base. The narrow-type container is more economical to use but do see that it is secure and not likely to tip over with tall foliage. Place the foliages in a safe cool clean area where they can slowly absorb the solution. Mark carefully if there is any doubt that someone may use them.

After a week or so, watch carefully for any change in foliage colour. Do not leave until the glycerine works its way through the leaf stomata because if you do you are left with a sticky surface which picks up all the dust. The thicker the leaves, the longer they take to treat. Watch the level of solution in the container. Keep this topped up. Once finished, bottle any left for another time.

Just one point to remember: the foliage must be at the correct stage when treating – not too young and certainly not late on in the season. Autumn colours are wonderful but these are brought about by a change of moisture and food content in the leaf. The plant food is automatically cut off in the autumn, which in turn causes leaf fall. By the time the colour of the leaf is changing, the supplies are being curtailed so should you place the stems in glycerine it will never reach the leaves. It is a pity that we cannot 'hold' autumnal colours. The only way to try is by pressing a few very colourful leaves to be used deep down in the vase and may be select some clever artificial sprays of foliage to make the outline to the vase.

PRESSING This is a simple and ideal way of holding flowers in perfect condition and retaining, in most cases, good colours. It is a good way of making a flower picture. A very good friend and old student has recently produced a book on this very subject which I would suggest you read. It is *Pressed Flowers* by Joanna Sheen, published by Merehurst Press.

You are, of course, limited to small amounts and only individual leaves or flower heads – not large sprays of foliage. You will need good-quality blotting paper, newspaper, corrugated paper and a press which is easy to work. Again, you should record contents and dates because this gives you an idea of how long things are taking. Those flowers with fleshy petals are the most difficult to do.

Once pressed, you can then make up on false stems and here I have to admit to the use of a glue-gun. I do not feel it correct to use in ordinary floristry – it seems to be cheating to me – but with stemless flowers it is an ideal way of fixing them.

Recently I saw an exhibition of paintings and flowers. The flowers themselves were mostly pressed but the stems and foliages were painted. It was most attractive and very realistic. I had to look twice to see which was real and what had been painted. There are some very clever people about and there will always be someone coming up with slightly different ideas. Try yourself when you have time – you may suddenly set a new fashion!

I said earlier that you could only press flower heads or individual leaves but I quite forgot another way of doing large fronds of fern. Take up your carpet and place full-size sheets of brown paper on the floor, then lay out fronds of the Royal Fern (Osmunda regalis) and Bracken, covering each piece with a sheet of newspaper, allowing up to four layers on top of each other. Ensure that the foliage is kept from touching. Cover with another layer of brown paper, then carefully replace the carpet. Leave this for 6–8 weeks and you will have perfectly-pressed and dried foliage for backing a large group. The movement of people over the carpet breaks down the thick stem structure but it seems to remain intact.

Arranging dried flowers

There are two problems when arranging dry flowers:
1) One is that the stems can be very brittle so the flower heads tend to snap off as you work with them.
2) You need to work well down into the vase because, having thin stems that are leafless, the base of the arrangement can look very bare and unattractive. It is here that those pressed or large leaves treated with glycerine come into use. One or two, well placed over the rim and through the centre of the vase, hide the mechanics.

Containers are no problem because all you need is something in keeping to hold the flowers. Stems may be placed at all angles without the worry of having to be in water, but still always ensure that they radiate from a centre point. Good, flowing lines make for well-balanced and natural-looking arrangements. My own feeling is that dried materials look best in the heavy-looking containers, such as pottery, wood, basketware and metal. I don't like glass and fine china, but you must use your common sense. For instance, a very dainty 'dried' could look perfect arranged in a piece of bone china to stand on a dressing table: an ideal gift for a birthday present.

You must always be thinking how to make attractive gifts. Something for a special present is nice especially if it will go on usefully once the flowers have finished their decorative life. I believe that if it is explained to the customers then they will appreciate the idea and be prepared to pay that little extra for a special container. It is when they know that once the flowers have finished the container will be discarded that problems of how much has been spent on the container arise. There is no reason why anything suitable cannot be used for dried material. Those vases with thin necks or the container that is cracked and no longer able to hold water safely will now come into their own. I believe that glass, unless it is old and of the right colour, is something to leave alone, as is modern silver; but heavy copper, brass, bronze and pewter will be useful if you get the correct colour combination. Very fine china does not seem correct to me but stoneware and heavy, dark pottery may be used in many different ways – that stone pot that contained Stilton at Christmas will be an ideal container.

Vases in alabaster are another lovely material to use with flowers – some of the pale types go well with pinks, mauves and grey, and the deeper yellow/fawn colours with the browns, rusts and greens. The tall, upright style of arrangement can look good in a home-made vase. Take a narrow, upright can (lager or soup) and remove the top cleanly leaving no sharp edges. Wash and dry well. Select a piece of wallpaper – such as a Japanese straw or a heavy, anaglipter type which will take a colour wash – and cover the tin surface neatly. A small band of velvet ribbon may be placed at the top and bottom to give a neat finish. When dry and ready to use, half fill with dry sand or gravel for weight and then top up with 2″ wire netting or a piece of Oasis *Sec* plus a little netting.

I can see an arrangement of Beech twigs with nuts attached, small Reed mace, Oats and grass seed heads, a group of dried or preserved Magnolia leaves at the base to break the hard line of the vase, and perhaps a few bronze heads of Helichrysum. Just simple materials arranged carefully can make a most pleasing group for an odd corner in the room. Select your colour for the wallpaper and its trimming and the flowers in the container. Skeleton Magnolia leaves would be better for the silver pinks, greys and blues and some upright bleached materials – even some white sprayed branches could be used. I feel strongly that over-arranging can spoil the effect that dried and preserved materials should give: simplicity should be the guideline to follow. You always have to rather overfill the vase to hide the bare stems unless, as I have suggested, a group of preserved leaves or something similar makes that 'focal point'.

The mechanics used in holding drieds are important. They should be backed up with something heavy in the base of the container to stop them from tipping over. The pinholder as such has no use here, but a 'frog' – that special pinholder with 4–5 pins only – may be a great help. This holds the Oasis *Sec* firmly. Never attempt to use an ordinary pinholder with any of the foam substances. The needles all become clogged up and the middle just falls away from the block of foam. I find dried silver sand as good as anything in conjunction with 2″ netting. It allows the thin dried stems to penetrate right down into the base of the vase giving excellent support. Once the framework of the stems is fixed, the other stems need only to be tucked in – no worry of being below the water-table!

Gravel gives the weight but does not allow the stems to penetrate far, and often they will snap off on touching the hard surface. A block of Oasis – both *Sec* for firm material and the normal Oasis for the more fragile stems – will give you extra holding-power than just wire netting. It gives you confidence, when arranging, if stems stay where you place them. Once you get into the swing, just wire netting in the top of the vase will be all that is necessary for working in the home. Certainly you will need something like Oasis if you are having to move the arrangements, for example when selling from a shop or making them to sell for a charity where they will be carried away.

If working with a framework of branches or something large, a lump of Dryhard or Plasticine may be the ideal medium in which to set up the framework, in conjunction with other support from netting or Oasis later on. With Dryhard you must work quickly in the early stages and then allow it to dry thoroughly before continuing on with the filling-in materials.

Table cracker in gold and silver

This decoration is constructed entirely from artificial material, so the pieces may be made well before the Christmas rush and stored ready to put together. The base is a cake board which may be covered in any chosen colour. The cracker is made up to the size you require in cardboard covered with crinkle paper. Ribbon and a bow pinch in the cracker end, which is made in two pieces. In the middle, place a piece of dry Oasis, covered in paper (tin foil is excellent). Arrange your fronds of plastic fern, flowers and baubles and bells in the Oasis base.

This may be done one sided or to be seen from all round; it is effective and easy to make.

9. Artificial decorations

Artificial flowers are not a new idea; there has always been a use for them and probably always will be. At first flowers carved both in stone and wood featured greatly in our old buildings. The very early stems were made of metal or a very stiff paper, and were painted in oil to colour and protect them. Then we see the addition of other forms of decoration. China flowers, and those made of plaster, also had a period when they were popular. The white flowers and foliages under glass domes which rested on graves as a form of a floral tribute are still seen in shrines and graveyards abroad.

In my travels with flowers to places on the other side of the world, I have been amazed to see all the different ways flowers are used in decorations, and perhaps some of the most striking are the mosaics made from broken pieces of coloured pottery and china on the walls of the old Royal Palace of Bangkok. The details here are quite outstanding. The wonderful stone carving on the forts and temples in India and the wood carvings on shrines in Nepal are also wonderful examples.

The use of shells and corals to make pictures is another form of decoration which has been practised for many years, and only recently has it become popular again. Many people forget that all these things have been done before, and in times when there were none of the aids we have today to help us.

Pictures and wall swags in dried materials are very popular. I hope the use of plastic flowers and foliage is now well on the way out, to be replaced with the so much more life-like ones in polyester and silk. I am always amazed to see plastic flowers and foliages used in wreathwork on the Continent, especially Switzerland. Graveyards often have many large tributes on display so any student working abroad will have to work with these. In fairness though, they do try to blend the colours and make the best use of them. Some of these are quite remarkable and if you are really selective and grade out the correct seasons and colours, a quite perfect group can be gathered together. These will serve a most useful purpose where weather conditions are not suited to using the real or living thing: in the theatre, for example, where it is not safe to have the chance of water being spilt, or in a basement devoid of any light for long periods where it would be just impossible for real plant growth. It is so important to get the correct shape and movement to the plants. When they are boxed up they are laid flat for ease of packing and this must be rectified and the stems brought to 'life' as soon as they are unpacked. Study the real plant growing and put this knowledge into your silk product.

Many years ago Constance Spry made the most beautiful artificial flowers, foliages and fruits. A few of these are still to be seen today, especially those covered in glass domes where they are free from dust and can be kept totally clean. These were perfect in every detail. Based on white crepe paper and cotton wool, they were all made from fresh living samples and hand-coloured, sometimes taking two to three different coats to get the colours right. The petals of living flowers were stripped down and a paper pattern made from each one to get the exact shape, then each was hand-painted. The wiring of these allowed for perfect shaping – the elasticity of the crepe paper allowing a little fullness to the blown Rose petals, for instance. After shaping, they were dipped in different forms of wax to get the correct textures and those that needed a soft, furry finish, such as on the skin of a Peach fruit, were processed yet again. This was a very long and costly process but they were so good that they went out all over the world and were used on many occasions by photographers unable to get the 'live' product. Having worked for many hours now with photographers, I know just how exacting their needs can be, so these artificial materials had to be good. Everything, we are told, progresses and now, if you have the money, anything in the fruit and vegetable line is available so the need dropped off for the wax products.

The biggest challenge we ever had was to make Dandelion clocks for a television programme at Christmas. The seeds, on their little parachutes, actually had to fly away when blown by two little children – a tricky problem but it worked. The girls making them spent many hours of research before they perfected them and to this day, although I watched the process of production, I do not know exactly how they finalised the dispersal of the seed parachutes.

The latest flowers and leaves are in acrylic. This looks like glass in black and white colours. They are very smart with clean-cut shapes, very stiff-looking with no movement and easy to wash; but a limited market I would think. They are only right in an ultra-modern setting and something that I would soon get very tired of looking at. Many new items come and go quite quickly, but it always makes sense to hold on to these ideas because you never know when they may be very useful. A dramatic window setting calls for some special bits. Where can you find them? Can I impress upon you when storing anything of this nature to label each box carefully, correctly and all in the same place for quick identification. How often have you been caught out knowing full-well that you have got something in store but cannot be sure where it is? Time costs money in trying to find it and it is certain that it will be in the last box that you look in!

Years ago, except for the hand-made flowers from Constance Spry, I would not have looked at, let alone use, artificial flowers. But today some of them are so good that you have difficulty in telling the difference unless you are quite close up. They are not cheap, but when you think about it, you can use them time and time again, if you keep them clean and well stored between times. They are a wonderful source of supply in a difficult time. I believe you should try to keep them seasonal; have supplies for the four seasons.

If you find difficulty in getting people to accept artificial flowers, try a few of one kind with real foliage as a background – you will have many people foxed. Once convinced they will enjoy the challenge of doing a really good, mixed group from time to time. I think the important factor is to get realistic colours – this is easy in the top-quality silks. When using polyester, you could go astray because some plant colourings are horrific.

To be really convincing, arrange silk just as you do your real flowers, grouping the different shapes and colours, and getting good, flowing lines at the sides and over the front of the vase. Proportion and balance, both visual and actual, apply just the same. Because the foliage can be difficult to obtain at times, plants such as a Begonia Rex may be useful low down at the front.

Containers

I believe that you can use most of the normal containers and many more – remember in some ways it is easier because there is not the worry of holding water to be considered, unless you are using fresh foliage. Although there are some charming little flowers in silk, many of the really large ones such as the Poppy and Paeony are very striking and require arranging in really large containers to look their best. Silk flowers are fairly lightweight but they can easily be knocked over, so the balance must be correct.

You can arrange in ordinary wire netting but with the thin, wiry stems you may need a few more layers and to have the wire higher in the vase for extra support.

Oasis *Sec* is fine for a small group but with many stems it tends to break apart. Some people use a small amount of Dryhard in the container in which to stick the stems. This will dry and become hard in a very short time. For foliage plants, a large deep bowl or copper pan filled with small gravel can be successful. If arranging artificial materials, we find using a ball of moss worked into some 2″ wire is ideal in the container. It is heavier than a block of Oasis *Sec*. For a really tall group, add washed gravel to the vase base.

Backgrounds are important to show off the flowers properly. They give the atmosphere to the setting and then the flowers should add to it rather than detract or stand apart. Natural settings are the best – do not try to be too clever and overdo it because it does not work. By covering up things that you wish to hide, sometimes they appear more prominent. A mirror can make a good background for some low groups but see that the back is well finished off and tidy. Also remember that a mirror multiplies the number of flowers needed in the arrangement, so do not overcrowd.

At one time, not so long ago, the use of anything artificial was really looked down upon and considered not the done thing. But today that attitude has changed and there are many different plants, foliages and flowers now on the market. I believe that there is a place for something artificial when and where fresh materials cannot be used. They are not new, in fact, artificial materials have been going for many years in various forms.

The best hand-made artificials were introduced by the late Constance Spry and were in use just before the war, but they were limited and costly. They were perfect for shape and colour, and in every detail correct. Each flower or leaf was made from cutting a pattern from the living material – a Pansy, for instance, was taken to pieces, petal by petal and templates of these petals were made and numbered. Markings and colourings were recorded so that the correct detail could be bound back together in the correct sequence – a time-consuming job but so worthwhile. Once every detail was worked out and the finished product appeared perfect, then a production line could be set up. Remember, however, that no two flowers are quite the same in shape or marking, so this must be seen in your product.

A green tazza, with mixed foliage and silk Poinsettia

This wide flat-footed vase lends itself to holding branches with fairly thick stems. It may be used for either a facing or an all-round arrangement. In this instance it has a piece of Oasis in the base and this is held firmly by one or two layers of wire netting secured with Oasis tape. This will hold everything well and allow plenty of room for water. A pinholder could equally well have been used had the base of the vase been flat, but this one has very curving sides. The materials have been chosen for a winter decoration and they should all be long lasting.

Fresh cut Poinsettia are not available except just prior to Christmas so we have used polyester/silk ones in this arrangement. The red of the coloured bracts picks up the red in the curtain stripe. If using the fresh flowers, the cut surface must be treated by burning the tip to seal it or placing it in boiling water for 30 seconds. Any leaf which is removed must also be sealed at its base to stop any bleeding and this is best done by holding over a candle flame for a few seconds. Once fresh Poinsettia take up water they last well but it is essential to prepare them properly. In this particular arrangement the bare stems of Cornus (dogwood) set the height with Osmanthus on the right and varieted holly (Ilex) on the left. Bare Larch (Larix) with cones Ivy (Hedera) both green berried and variegated, Spotted Laurel (Aucuba), Blue Cedar (Cedrus atlantica), and the Holly-leaved Osmanthus are also to be seen in the mixed collection of long-lasting foliages.

To help hide the mechanics, place some moss (bun moss or Reindeer moss) on top of the vase and push the stems through it. It will dry naturally and looks good for a long time. Once dry spray with hair lacquer or glue to hold the moss together.

If working with pot plants (and some of the silk plants are very good), you can make the soil look most realistic. First set the stem in Dryhard or a block, then get some dry peat which is well broken down. Mix this with a little hot paraffin wax to make it into good potting 'soil'. Add to the top of the pot and allow to set. Do not pat down – leave rough but well spread over the whole surface.

Once seen, these flowers were in demand for use by photographers who were working with fruits and flowers out of season, as they so often have to do. There has never been anything to touch them, but today the price inhibits their use in large numbers. They are still made to order. (See note at back of book for detail.) The modern silk/polyester flowers, provided they are the correct colour, can be most realistic. When well-arranged and given the correct movement and shape so that they look natural, there are places where they could pass for the real thing. The important point is not being able to get too close. Another very important detail to remember is to keep them fresh-looking and clean. Just because they do not drop pollen or loose a few petals in the first week does not mean that they do not want attention. By keeping them dusted all the time you will soon see when washing is necessary. So often it is the foliage that lets them down and, with many silk flowers, the stems and foliages are made of a substance which cannot be washed – a drawback and something you must note with care.

I believe one of the most useful ways to use artificial flowers is in conjunction with fresh foliage. In the late winter period, when flowers are very expensive and the fresh spring flowers are fairly short-stemmed and only lasting a few days, I cannot but agree to attaching artificial Camellia flowers to the living foliage. I know it is expensive and I am never sure how people can bring themselves to cut large branches of Camellia foliage, but it is worth every penny because it does last well in water. The foliage is a lovely green with a glossy sheen to the leaf surface and lends itself to having the flowers attached firmly to the growing tips of the branches. If you study the living plant you will notice where most of the flowers are carried and you should copy this pattern. The flowers are held on very short stems so the fixing should be easily hidden under the flower itself – either bind on with a little wire, covered with a band of gutta percha, or glue on. This is the method in vogue at present – it is most effective. The Camellia is a very waxy-looking flower so lends itself to being made in a fabric, which is coloured and then waxed. The most common colour is red, pink and white so can easily be copied. The style of flower ranges from single, with a mass of stamen, through semi-double to a double.

Another wonderful flower, quite easy to make, is the Magnolia. It varies in size, shape and colour but most are cup-shaped, again on very short stems, so you do not have the problem of making artificial stems which I find are so often a real problem in man-made materials. The flowers come out before the foliage in the spring-flowering varieties, so you only have to find the correctly shaped branches on which to attach them.

Anything with a waxy texture is good to copy. The other flower which can go onto living foliage, which is long-lasting and readily available, is the Rhododendron. The flowers are quite easy to make and the colours are good to copy – white, cream, pink to red. Some flowers have spots or various markings, which must be added to the throat of the flower to make them more realistic. The individual stems are thin and have to be bound together to form the flower cluster which is then attached to the foliage as a terminal group – just as the natural flowering Rhododendrons appear in the garden.

All these types mentioned would last three to four weeks which would take you through a difficult period after the New Year. I remember so well when we did decorations on a weekly contract basis. Those flowers close to the public eye had to be fresh and sweet-smelling but those decorations out of reach, but still showing well and where colour was necessary, could often be arrived at with artificials for a short period of time. As I said before, artificials are expensive to set up but, lasting for three to four weeks, would balance out favourably on the financial side.

This leads me to an entirely 'artificial' group. Do try to keep to seasonal flowers – a difficult and controversial subject today with so many flowers coming in from all round the world. The true season has gone if you really think about it when marketing these days. I still like to think of the four seasons; winter, spring, summer and autumn.

The winter season can be helped with an outline of branches, covered in Lichen and some wonderful sprays of Larch with those pretty cones attached – a decoration in themselves. Alder with immature catkins and cones will dry well also for the outline. Make a framework of these subjects and wire up some large sprays of Magnolia leaves (dried or preserved) and perhaps a few large cones for the centre of the group. Some seed pods, such as Poppy and Reed

Mace, would give another shape. Then add a few flowers, for example, large Chrysanthemums well placed, or cut Poinsettia, because both these are well made in polyester. I can picture this as I write; I hope you can also! More dried materials could be used, but the simple lines of my first suggestion should be enough. I do like simplicity and everything to show up well.

Somehow the spring is not so easy to do. So many of the flowers are short and would not fit into a large group. A basket of moss with small clusters of plant or bulbs can look quite pleasing and authentic. I would suggest here that a 'Dutch Group' or a 'Dutch Master' would be an excellent idea to try. First you must choose the correct type of vase – something bold, heavy and rather squat-like in metal or stone. There are many pictures which you may try to imitate. All are so attractive and lend themselves to silk flowers. It is just a matter of having the right types of stems or suitable substitutes. I normally would work with a ball of wire netting in which I had rolled some moss. This is slightly damp and holds the stems well. The modern Oasis Premium would also work well with just a layer of wire netting over the block to hold it firmly in place. I know many people, especially those doing flowers commercially, just use the block of Oasis on its own but I prefer to have the support of the wire which is raised slightly above the vase rim.

You will notice in any traditional Dutch flower painting the lack of foliage. The bold flowers seem to be more dominant when not over-shadowed by leaves. Also one or two very heavy flowerheads come right into the outline of the vase. They break our rules, or guidelines, and get away with it! Always a difficult point to put over with students who never miss a chance to query what you may be doing. We tend to suggest that the largest or heaviest-looking flowers go to the centre of the vase and every time I see those wonderful paintings I wonder how they have succeeded in getting the correct visual balance. Study the pictures yourself; I find many seem to be slightly square in outline and inclined to be very full of flowers. How I wish I could copy them and get away with it!

Again, the seasons are often very wide because they have painted them over a long period. They are not copied from a fresh group of flowers but built up on the canvas as the work progressed.

If you succeed in arriving at a group which imitates the style of a painting by a Dutch Master you may keep it for many months provided it remains clean and fresh-looking, but you cannot keep your spring basket of Narcissi and Polyanthus or your Tulips throughout the summer.

Now let's turn to the summer group. There are some lovely sprays of Roses which are very realistic. Some even have large Hips attached which all make for interest, so I feel you can go for these in a big way. The Rose is something very much associated with England and the English garden and to have them lasting a little longer without dropping their petals is such an advantage! How you get round the scent is your problem but there are perfumes that you can add to make them more authentic. For my last book, *Dried and Artificial Flower Arranging* (Octopus), I did an arrangement of mixed roses, but somehow I feel I would prefer that to be kept to the Hybrid Tea types. When using the wider range of singles and ramblers. I would like more restraint on the colour range – say cream, apricots to yellows or perhaps a range of soft pinks, mauves, greys and silvery purple with the appropriate foliage. There is such a wide choice today that you can experiment endlessly.

The autumn is more straightforward. Autumnal colourings in fruit, berries, seed heads and a range of flowers make an excellent group – something which you may enjoy for two to three months and before you know where you are Christmas is upon you.

As a grower at heart, I love my fresh materials but when flowers are short, dried materials are useful. But every year as the Fancy Goods Fair comes round and new artificial materials become available, I am more convinced that there is a need and a place for these flowers. Do try them – I am sure that they will 'grow' on you, not at the expense of growing or fresh-cut flowers but for places where the latter may not be used happily.

Artificial flowers and foliage are not easy to wire because there is so little chance of hiding the wire. In fresh material, many flowers have soft, succulent or hollow stems so the wire can be hidden internally. In artificial materials, everything has to be wired externally so in most cases artificial stems of wires are made which can be bound with a green gutta to make them look stem-like. Again, securing the end of a wire into a natural seed box is ideal. It supports the base of the flower and makes the ideal starting point for the wire down the stem. In artificials, the seed box is non-existent so you have to hide the wire end, suitably secured into the base of the flower petal.

10. *Planning and procedures*

There is a lot of planning involved when working on any project. Let me go through a rough programme which you might have to follow.

You may get involved because you have said 'yes' to a request to supply the flowers, or you may have had your name suggested by a firm that recommended that you should do the job. Anyhow, once your name has been chosen you must visit the site of the forthcoming occasion so that you can get an idea of what will be wanted on the day. If you are giving the flowers you will say what you feel you can supply. If you are asked for suggestions and ideas, you must estimate the cost. Before arriving on site you will have booked an appointment – keep to the time and meet the person or persons concerned with a note-book ready to take down all the details. It is important to appear business-like and allay any fears of incompetence. It may be the first time that you have been involved in a job of this nature but remember everyone has to make a start at some time or another.

Visiting the place to be decorated

As you take down notes, remember that there will be a strict time-schedule and there may be rehearsals or services to avoid, so plan carefully in your mind the time it will take to do the job. When estimating, always allow a little extra time, because something always crops up to hinder you while you are working.

The Constance Spry School were involved with flowers for the 900th anniversay of Domesday in Westminster Abbey. The commemorative service was to take place in the presence of Her Majesty the Queen Mother. We met one of the clergy responsible for the flowers, and he informed us where we could place the flowers on this occasion and how the people would be seated for the service. We were asked to give names and addresses to persons doing the work on the day also to state vehicles we would be using with the registration numbers. Duty passes were duly sent to us to cover the days we would be working and for an early visit for checking on the actual day of the service. Parking permits to enable a close approach to the 'Deans Yard' where a trolley could be used to transport the vases, bases and large boxes of foliage and flowers through the cloisters and up to a side entrance by the choir stalls. At the same time I did ask for permission to have a professional photographer in and this was granted so more passes were needed for these people. At that point it was the right stage at which to write and confirm everything, at the same time sending a copy of the letter to the organisation asking you to carry out the work so that they are in the picture about what is going on.

Even if the occasion for which you are preparing is a far more humble one than this, proper preparation and thinking ahead are vital if you are to succeed. A lack of communication on anyone's part can lead to disaster, and timing is so important. The way that you organise yourself and tackle the job makes a big impression on the people in charge; for example, untidy work means that it takes twice as long to clear up afterwards.

As you go round, do it systematically so that later on you can make a rough sketch and work it all out without the chance of missing anything. Make copious notes and detail colours to be picked up and any special items that may strike you.

In church, remember that the wall colouring will make a big difference to the flower colours showing up – blues and mauves will be lost at a distance when in front of a grey stone wall. Take notice of any lighting: spot-lights trained on to a group really do work wonders. Any flowers to be on ledges or window-sills will have to be in the right containers, so get overall measurements and maximum sizes for the vase base so that everything will be safe. Make notes on how the vases may be secured. List vases on your notes to help identify each group and which type of pedestal should be used in each place.

Another request that often comes up is for garlanding and this does take a long time to make and may be difficult to set up. First you must have permission for fixing it which is always a problem. Often in an old church the pillars are not all the same size and the addition of garlands exaggerate this fact rather than take from it. I am not a garland person – I would rather have the money for garlands spent on another beautiful group.

I was once asked to do the flowers for a wedding taking place in a very ornate church in Surrey. The carvings at the back of the altar, and vase screen dividing the choir stalls from the main body of the church looked like an exhibit of fretwork – it was beautifully done. At the back of the church was another large archway and the cover for the font was a vast eight-sided wooden pinacle. Every edge of every curved arch (some 80 feet on the front alone) had to be covered with garlands of Carol Roses and silver foliage. Garlanding was not my favourite subject before, but after this I was definitely off it! After many hours of work, the pretty garland only really showed up when you were close to it. Three large groups would have done very much more for the church and I believe would have enhanced the screen as a superb background.

As you work your way to the back of the church, remember to suggest a group to be seen as the guests leave. Quite often, you will find the font at the back of a church and provided it is allowed, you may find a large all-round group will stand up well here. Flowers must not be arranged in the font but on it, so that they can be removed should a christening be taking place while your decorations are in the church. A large wash basin or mixing bowl is ideal for this position.

I would suggest you ask to see the vases and plinths belonging to the church, so that if they were at all suitable you may use them rather than have to carry all your own. Plinths are heavy and take up a lot of room when travelling.

Remember that you will work better with your own vases than with ones with which you are not familiar. Make a careful note of what is to be supplied by the church and their position, at the same time noting what you must supply.

After going to see a job, I always prefer to come back to the office and quickly add some more notes, so that should I be lucky enough to get the job, everything will be easy to follow. It is so important to make notes and really get the correct vases and stands to suit the surroundings.

Make notes on parking and unloading space, and how you reach your destination. Should you not be doing the job on the day, then this will help the person doing it for you. Sometimes you may be involved in a special job with a VIP in attendance and then things will be more difficult. You will have to supply the authorities with registration details of vehicles used and names and addresses of persons helping with the decorations.

You should get your work photographed when doing special commissions so that you will have records to show people later on. This may be difficult and expensive, but it is very worthwhile. I have decided that you should never miss an opportunity because it may never crop up again. Often we said, 'we will do it next time' and then find that we could have used the photographs had we had some.

Supplying an estimated cost

People will expect estimates quite quickly unless you are in the happy position of being guaranteed the job. You should give a detailed estimate so that each item shows up and then if, for some reason, it is decided necessary to cut back, it can be done easily. Remember you can suggest certain flowers but always cover yourself by saying 'if available', remembering to let them know what you are proposing to substitute should the first choice be not forthcoming on the day. Do not ever allow the possibility for a complaint. Everyone tends to be a little up-tight on special occasions and you do not want to be the one to upset things.

As you do your estimate, you should list the flowers you feel that you will want in each group; if doing pairs all you have to do is double up. By recording the foliage, then any spike shapes for height, the main flowers for the centre, and those over the sides to give some flow, then the 'filling in', you will get a good overall picture. Do not forget the time of year for the decoration. Once you have one or two large groups it all comes into line. The usual thing is to get in far too much material. Keep your arrangements light and open, so that every flower shows up in its own right. Do not get too many different colours and shapes because at a distance these all tend to merge into a rather dense mass.

Once the estimate is accepted you can make your provisional market list. So much can happen during a very short time which may necessitate a change to your list. Weather and growing conditions will cause prices to fluctuate. Even a foggy morning can throw you when supplies do not get to the market. Supply and demand still fixes the basic price.

Your percentage mark-up will depend entirely on your overheads and where you are working. Do not be too greedy but see that everything is covered and

Mixed garden roses in a white tazza

These lovely mixed roses are arranged in a marble tazza and are standing in the window looking out into the conservatory. They are of all types, massed together for scent and colour, but as you will be able to see, none are perfect blooms because of the inclement weather conditions that particular year. Remember, as they open they will spread, so leave space when arranging. Do not over-arrange the flowers – allow them to fall naturally into place. Keep the flower petals afterwards; they will go towards a pot-pourri.

you have a profit on everything that you do. Some things will be better than others and you take the rough with the smooth. Remember also that any prices quoted in the market never include VAT and any secondary buyer charges a percentage for getting material for you. It all adds up! It takes a long time to get a good name but you quickly get a bad name which stays with you for a long time. Life is very competitive these days and value for money is important.

About a week before the job is due to be done, it is worth asking about the materials you will need. In fact, any special items should have been discussed well before this to give your salesman a chance to get the right things for you. Do remember when estimating that there are certain times when prices go up. Mothering Sunday and the Jewish New Year come to mind straight away, so these must be brought into consideration. It is no good saying it does not happen because it does. Nobody misses a trick these days if they are good business people.

Organising the work

Time flies when you are busy and soon the forthcoming occasion will be with you. Depending on its size you will assess the number of helpers you need. But whatever you do, do not take too many people with you. A few hard-working members of staff will get it done so much quicker and better than when you have people falling over themselves. Another point to remember is not only do you have to transport and pay them, but the person employing you to do the job is not going to be impressed either.

Everything should have a good drink the day before travelling and then it can either travel in buckets of water or laid flat in boxes. Much will depend on the size of vehicles you are using. We always pick out the flowers for each group and label them so that they are ready to be given out straight away when arriving on the job. The main foliage may have to travel all in one but if this can also be allocated out for the different groups, it all saves so much time, and often cuts down the mess factor too. To look and be efficient makes such a good impression. When packing in boxes, you will be able to pack in pairs or say different groups on the window sills. It is essential to keep each one divided so that everyone gets their fair share when they start arranging.

When doing pairs of vases you may like to work in pairs or some people prefer to work on their own. However it is done it is important to get the foliage in first to match, set the same height and width by standing well back in the church or hall. By dividing up first you will stand a better chance of getting similar-looking vases. I have in the past found people doing groups from boxes and heaps of flowers on the ground without any thought of what they can use, only to find at the end, the last few vases are very sparse. Be fair with yourself and your colleagues, but remember the most important vases must have the special things in them.

If you have a long distance ahead of you, you may be able to load up the evening before. In this case the flowers and foliage would be better in buckets, so that an early start can be made. Leave the dustsheets until last to go on, or wrap each large vase or plinth in them for protection, but remember they will be needed first.

On arrival at the job, first lay out a dustsheet at the various places where flowers are to be used, one for each decorator, then place the plinths and vases in position. There will be no problem here because all are marked. Lastly carry the buckets or boxes into a central bank in the building, standing them all on another dustsheet. Allocate a vase to each decorator if they have not already been told. They can then collect their bucket and go forward to the job. If foliage is to come from a central bank this will be on another dustsheet. See that they share this out carefully – you can not afford to run out.

As one vase is completed, so you move on to another, taking your main rubbish with you. If you have an extra pair of hands (non-decorator) with you, here is where the final cleaning up and topping up of water can be done which is a great help. It is always difficult to say how much time a group will take. Sometimes a very large one is quicker to do than a smaller one. Different decorators will certainly differ in their speed, but you will know this from working with them before.

People can sometimes be extremely kind on these occasions and expect you to sit down to a large lunch. This is a lovely idea but when you are really busy and working against time, it is much better for all concerned to just accept a plate of sandwiches or something similar and really to work on. Rules and regulations (guaranteed lunch hours) on these occasions go to the wall. You will have plenty of time to sit quietly on the way home especially if you are lucky enough to have a driver.

Clean up as you work. Possibly you will have started your work the furthest away from your supplies, so after each vase you should bring back the rubbish near to base. A last look round and spray over should set everything up. All you can do is hope for a cool night and that no problems occur before the function the next day.

Arrangements must be checked over the next morning, topped up again with water and any stems that happen to have gone down should be replaced. With luck nothing will have happened, but if you are not prepared you may need something. The length of time the flowers have to last will depend on the function. For example, it may be a flower festival or a very special series of music recitals when flowers will be needed for a period of time. Three to four days is the maximum period for flowers to last in prime conditions, but with careful maintenance, a week should be achievable. A hot, dry atmosphere, smoke-filled rooms, and full sun and drying winds all play havoc and will sadly shorten the life of the flowers. Hardy foliage, such as Camellia, will last three to four weeks but it will be very much more expensive to purchase in the first place. All this will have to be worked out beforehand and this is where the experience comes in.

Always take your rubbish away with you, unless told to do otherwise. Arrange to leave somewhere on the site a reserve bucket of flowers, just in case of problems. They will be better on site rather than travelling up and down in your vehicle.

Clearing the work

Again, this should be done in a business-like manner. Some people say that they will do this and have everything ready for you to collect at a certain date. I have even known of the odd occasions when all the vases and plinths have been returned by the client. If this has been suggested and you can spare the time that the vases are away from your business, it will naturally cut the cost to the client (travelling and labour hours). Remember that you will have a book recording each item used so you can easily check it off as it is returned. There are times, however, when you are not so lucky so you need to have a system worked out.

Go to the farthest group from your vehicle taking a bucket with a little water, a large dustsheet, and dustpan and brush. Remove any good flowers (remember they have been paid for) and stand them in the bucket. Strip out the rubbish and then if any good foliage remains, keep it in a bunch. Carry on to the next group after brushing up the area. Go to each group in turn, arriving back at base with any good flowers in water, all the rubbish in the dustsheet, and good foliage laid on top. Now go back with a bucket and empty all the vases of water. Then carry the empty vases back to the van (carry a cloth for occasional spills). Lastly, collect the plinths. This is a job that a good driver could do because it wants a strong, responsible person but not necessarily a florist.

Give your detailed account to the client straight away. Any adjustments that have occurred in the estimate will have been noted separately. Perhaps the daily topping-up, for instance, has been done 'in house' so did not incur that extra cost. Charity functions always want to know the final figure as soon as possible so they will be pleased to hear from you.

One good job leads to another, so it is of the utmost importance that you give your best on every occasion. You learn something on every occasion. It would make sense to take notes of each job of work done and list the 'watch points' as they occur.

Do's and don'ts with church flowers

Don't move any furnishings without asking first.

Don't hammer nails into pews or brickwork to hold flowers.

Don't remove flowers from anywhere without checking who did them and if they are wanted elsewhere. If they are still wanted but poorly done, try to hide them away in a side chapel so that they do not detract from your work.

Don't arrange flowers directly into the font.

Do get times of services before embarking on any major job; you should not carry on working whilst a service is in progress so try to work out your schedule around the service times.

Do tidy up as you go, and work in an orderly manner causing as little disruption as possible.

Do keep clean and tidy, and always work on a dustsheet.

Do make detailed arrangements in advance with the vicar and the secretary or leader in charge of flower arrangements in that particular church.

Gentians on rock crystal

The gentian is greatly under-estimated as a florist's flower and I feel this is really a 'creative' idea making it into a posy bouquet. Set up on rock crystal this alpine flower really looks at home. Edelweiss and silver grey foliage add the finishing touch, with the strong blue ribbon.

11. Weddings

*F*lower arrangers and florists will occasionally be asked to do things which they may consider a little out of the normal run of the business. So I am giving you an example and warning you of the problems that can occur.

Many years ago I was on duty on a Saturday morning and a very charming Dutch lady came into the shop. She explained that she lived just outside London and that her niece would be getting married from her home later in the year. The niece had been promised, as a wedding present, to have all her flowers sent over from Holland. The problem was, could anyone from Constance Spry arrange them and how could she go about it? Now I know today with so many flower clubs and church flower guilds actively running that this would be no problem. Someone would be sure to know someone who she was sure helped another person to do the flowers and this could be quickly followed up, but some 20 years ago it was a very different story.

My immediate reaction was to say yes. No one turns away work. Of course we could organise one of our decorators to do this, but we must follow the usual pattern of events. All that we would have to do was to visit the church and the home where the reception was taking place and see what was involved. A day and convenient time was fixed and I duly arrived with my note book to record all the details.

We first looked at the church – a rather modern and austere-looking building – and after a lot of discussion decided on six large groups with another in the entrance, and a small bowl on the vestry table. There were no stained glass windows or any colours to pick up so we could clearly choose any flowers. There were no window sills or ledges on which to stand vases and the suggestion of pew ends did not really appeal. Dutch churches and home interiors are somewhat plain and clear of a lot of material so I could see straight away that this would be too busy an effect for them. Two altar vases and pedestals were available for use in the church but there was no other equipment. All this detail was recorded.

Now it was the turn of the house, which was actually just behind the church. In fact, it would be arranged that we should park in the church car park instead of the busy road, and that a few feet of the garden fence should be removed to enable us to carry the flowers from the van to the garage the short way down the garden path.

As usual, I suggested a welcoming group in the hall and then we went into the large lounge where the wedding party was to receive the guests. This was a typical Dutch room with masses of plants, in perfect condition, placed along the window-sills. There would have to be little furniture adjustment on the day and it was decided one group would be behind the receiving line. It would make a wonderful backdrop for the shots of the bride.

The French doors led in to the garden where a small marquee would be erected. This was to be set up on the lawn with a small corridor to link it to the lounge. The striped lining, in primrose and white, would pick up the autumnal colours of the flowers. Two hanging baskets between the poles and lanterns on the walls at specific places would suffice. No table bowls were necessary as there was only to be a small sitting-out area. Flowers up high are all that are seen when people are standing. The wedding cake would be standing on a special cake table so a small amount of garlanding would be necessary in loops around the edge of the table plus a few posies, and to finish it off well a small fresh cake top would be ideal in a little silver vase.

Flowers would be placed in a bedroom, which was to be used as a cloakroom and a special arrangement was needed on the dining-room table for a family dinner party after the wedding was over. This was all that was required. The home was to look as natural as possible.

Then came the planning of the flower operation and this is where it could be tricky. All flowers for make-up work need to be a little more open than those arranged in vases. Remember, once flowers are out of water and wired they will not go on developing so I suggested that those that we would be using in the make-up work would be obtained by us from our usual market suppliers. We would as far as possible buy Dutch on this occasion.

It was very clear to me that the family would take care in preparing and conditioning all the flowers sent straight to them from Holland and I agreed to draw up all the contents for each vase and make up the complete list of requirements. At the same time I promised to supply a number of deep buckets which they would place in the garage to hold the flowers until we arrived to do the decorating.

On returning to the office I carefully worked out the costings for the decorations and the time and work involved. These were sent off and it was not long before we had a letter of acceptance, with a postscript saying that everything had been tied up in Holland, and everyone was longing for the day when we would start the decorations. We had agreed that I, and my fellow decorator, would come over the day before, with a final check for topping-up, delivery of the bouquets and setting-up the cake table in the morning of the wedding.

The moral of this rather long-winded story is: do *not* forget the weather when materials are coming from abroad. You must remember that this could cause everything to go wrong. This time it was fog and a sudden strike on the boats from Holland. The make-up side was covered – all materials were to hand – so there was no hold-up in this section; but the cut flowers were a great problem. It was not until about 7.30 pm on the night before the wedding that the flowers showed up. There was no time to prepare them. We started arranging them in really warm water – these were the house flowers which we could carefully watch. Those for the church were prepared by the family and went into buckets of warm water and we agreed to be at the church really early to cope with these the next morning. I was given accommodation for a very short night. After a very hectic morning, with one of the family collecting the make-up work from the London workroom, we had just enough time to have everything finished at the last moment.

Spring wedding

CURVED HAND SHOWER   The hand shower is made up of: Euonymus, Senecio Greyi, Hebe, variegated Ivy, cream Hyacinth, cream Freesia, Bahama Roses.

The Euonymus and Senecio Greyi leaves are wired on 32 swg double leg mounts and guttared, then sprayed up in twos, threes and fives mounted on a 22 swg × 10, 12 and 14″ wire.

The Hebe stem is cut short and wired with a loop at the base of the foliage and a double leg mount (a 32 swg silver wire is used). Gutta. The pieces can be sprayed up or left singly.

Variegated Ivy leaves – single stitch, double leg mount using 32 swg silver wire. Mount on a 24 or 22 swg × 10in;.

The Hyacinth is pipped and wired on a 32 swg silver wire. Guttared and sprayed up in twos, threes and fives on a 24 or 22 swg wire. Lengths of wires can vary. Keep the smallest flower to the top of the wire, largest to the bottom.

The cream Freesia looks best when left as natural as possible. Wire down in between the buds with a 36 or 32 swg silver binding wire. Cut the stems approx. 1″ under the last flower. Pierce a 22 swg wire up the inside of the stem and secure with the binding wire. Gutta.

The Roses are the main flower. Vary the lengths of the stems. The smallest flower will have the longest stem and the fullest flower will be cut very short so it can be tucked in deep in the bouquet. The 22 swg wire is pierced up the inside of the stem, through the seedbox to the base of the head. A 32 swg silver wire is used to secure the wire in place at the bottom of the stem. Gutta.

It is a good idea to stand the flowers up in vase once they are wired. This stops the heads getting bruised. The old idea was to use a moss pot. A flower pot packed with moss in which the wires were stuck by the apprentices ready for those to use when making up. The bouquet is bound together with a 32 swg silver binding wire.

To begin the bouquet attach the wire approximately 7″ from the top of the longest flower – this keeps the tail more flexible. So many bouquets look too stiff and rigid-looking often due to incorrect binding.

The tail needs to be pointed and the bouquet gradually widens as you reach the centre. To get the curve, build up on one side much more than the other. Obviously this depends on which side the curve is required. On the inside curve the flowers are kept very short. A few flowers and leaves need to be placed on the middle of the tail, keeping the light flowers for the outline.

The binding wire should travel at an angle until the centre is reached and then the binding wire is kept in one place. The tail is between 9–12″ long. When the centre is reached, this is the widest point in the bouquet.

The handle can now be bent or kept straight. The returned end is placed into position next. The length is approximately half the tail. It is bent back over the handle towards the short side of the bouquet. Firstly put in the outline working round to the widest point, then fill in the centre, varying all the lengths so that each flower can be seen clearly. The foliage should come through the bouquet and not be used just in the outline. Make sure the bouquet sits comfortably in the hand. The handle would be finished as other bouquets.

Spring wedding

Curved hand shower

This includes:
Euonymus, Senecio Greyi, Hebe, Variegated Ivy, cream Hyacinth, cream Freesia,
Behama Roses.

Bridesmaid's basket

Comb

Hebe, Ivy, Hyacinth and small yellow roses

Corsage

Small yellow roses on natural stems with foliage

BRIDESMAID'S BASKET Ribbon the handle with 1″ ribbon. In this case we have used an apricot colour. Attach two bows at the base of the handle.

As this basket has a flat bottom, place a piece of polythene on the wicker base. Then a small square of soaked Oasis. Attach this down with a piece of wire netting over it. Use a silver wire to secure it in position. The mechanics must be very firm.

The Hyacinths are wired as for a bouquet. The foliage can be wired or left on natural stems. Set the outline shape first. The arrangement should be light and dainty. Keep the front pieces well down and make sure the handle can be seen and there is room to hold the basket. Look into the sides of the basket and tuck a few flowers in round the back. It is a good idea to match the basket flowers with the ones being used in the bride's bouquet.

COMB Wire the materials – Hebe, Ivy, Hyacinth and small yellow roses – on 32 swg silver wire, double leg mounts and gutta:
Bind the spray together with a 36 swg silver wire.

The spray can be made up as a corsage and bound onto the comb or the materials can be bound straight onto the comb. Keep it light and dainty and make sure all the wires are bound in on the top of the comb so that there are no protruding wires to scratch the head.

The ribbon bow colour should match the bridesmaid's basket handle.

CORSAGE Small yellow roses on natural stems with foliage.

Wire down the stems with a 32 swg silver wire. Wire the leaves on a 32 or 36 swg silver wire. Gutta base.

Attach the 36 swg binding wire approximately 2″ from the top of the smallest bud. Place in a leaf behind. Gradually build out as you work down to the centre. The binding wire travels down at an angle. Work down approximately 2–3″ from the start of the binding wire. Keep the binding in one place and add in the width and a small returned end.

Remove the wires up to the binding point. Cut the stems to natural lengths. Trim the wires away.

Secure the binding wire and cut off. Gutta over the binding point. Place in a pin to the binding point so this can be attached to the outfit.

Flowers for the wedding

I have recently come across some notes written by the late Constance Spry on wedding flowers and I fould them most interesting. You always keep an eye open for new ideas in these changing days but I felt that it is worth quoting from her notes because she was so forward-thinking yet seemed to be so correct with all that she designed.

This is some of what she had to say. 'At one time, flowers for the wedding were looked on more as pretty accessories than as part of the pageant, but nowadays the bouquets and headdresses, the flowers for the church and the reception are all considered as part of the artistic scheme for the occasion. If they are not so considered and the bride's dress, the bridesmaids dresses and the flowers they wear or carry bear no relation to one another in style, colour or period – the occasion loses it dignity and beauty. To have beautiful flowers does not necessarily involve spending a lot of money: the simplest and least expensive kinds can give a beautiful effect if they are used properly.'

She goes on to say that technical skills and originality are needed in the design and that bouquets can be made of quite unusual flowers. This is something that I feel we miss out on today. There are infinite possibilities to choose from throughout the year and there is always scope for an individual approach as well as the conventional one.

The notes go on as follows: 'Bouquets may vary in shape as well as in content. You may have them made round or crescent shaped, or if you prefer it, in the form of a shapely hand-spray which, with its trailing effect, is becoming to most dresses and is easy to carry gracefully. There is a pitfall to avoid – gimmicky ideas! – one Lily or Daisy and a ribbon for example. I have seen stunts tried – the less said about them the better.'

Head-dresses of fresh flowers, as long as they are designed to suit the wearers, add greatly to the charm of a wedding. They should be on the simplest lines and not too large. They must be full, to show up well, but I would recommend control if they are to look correct.

In the church, the flowers should be part of the general colour scheme; unrelated masses will never give the right effect. You should make sure that they are well placed as groups of colour and, at the same time, that each vase is arranged so that it looks good in itself, and in such a way that it does not hide good architectural features in the church. There are sometimes rules as to where flowers may or may not be placed in a particular church, so it is as well to find out about these before making a plan. The attention of the wedding guests will of course be fixed in the direction of the altar. Generally speaking then, one good position for flowers is on each side of the chancel steps. Low groups will probably not be seen except by people in the front pews. On the other hand, outstanding vases on plinths will be better seen by the whole congregation, and will be a framework for the bride and bridegroom, and their attendants.

The reception, particularly when it is in a private house, gives a greater chance for variety than the church. The groups are to make a background for the bride and groom and should be in keeping with the bride's dress and her bouquet, but the flowers in the rest of the house can be chosen to suit individual rooms. Often, groups of foliage will go with the room just as well as flowers. The house is likely to be rearranged in any case, and it is probable there will be more opportunity to put flowers or foliage – perhaps where an important piece of furniture usually stands – in such a position that they will catch the eye. The best group naturally goes to make the background for the bride and groom at the point where they meet their guests, but it is a good idea to have a bowl or vase of flowers where the guests are waiting to congratulate them.

I think it is wise, when you consider the flower arrangements for the wedding to keep to a carefully-considered and simple plan throughout and, above all, to avoid anything that tends towards a fussy, inelegant show.

Summer wedding

This photograph shows a range of suitable wedding flowers and foliages available during the month of August.

Cabbage rose

Three or four open roses are needed for this spray.

Bride's bouquet

The bouquet includes: Geranium (green crispum and oak leaf), Tradescantia zibrina, Chlorophytum, Fern nephrolensis, Boston Fern, Stephanotis, roseta (pale pink rose), Bride gladioli, large white gladioli.

Victorian posy

The posy includes: Roseta, Sedum spectabile (green before changing to pink), Tweedia, pink statice, Brodiaea, white stock, pink carnation.

Parasol

The parasol is made up of: Hebe, blue Hydrangea, Cornflowers, cream statice, Senecio greyii.

Corsage

The corsage is composed of: Heather, geranium leaves, Hosta.

A summer wedding

CABBAGE ROSE   Three to four open Roses are needed for this spray.

Remove the petals from the Rose carefully. Keep one of the seed pods. Remove the sepals and cut the stem to approx. ¼". Wire with a 22 swg × 7" up the inside of the stem to the base of the head and secure with a 32 swg silver wire. Gutta over the natural stem and approximately 3" of the 22 swg wire. The petals are pleated, some singly and others in twos. Grade the petal sizes, and use a 32 swg silver wire. Some petals are on double legs and the others are on single leg mounts. The wires do not have to be guttared.

Wire 3 or 5 single Rose leaves with a single-stitch double leg mount, using 32 swg silver wire. If necessary extend the mounts. Gutta. Also wire approximately 7 small leaves to be used as backing leaves.

To make the spray attach the 36 swg binding wire under the stem of the Rose. Keep the binding in one place. Start with the small petals close to the stamens and graduate out to the larger ones. As the Rose increases in size the petals are placed on further away from the binding point. This spray should look like a full blown rose. Place the large leaves around the rose to look attractive. Now place on the small leaves in reverse to hide the wires. Cut the wires to approximately 2½ in. Bind down. Gutta.

BRIDE'S BOUQUET   Geranium (green Crispum), Geranium (Oak leaf), Tradescantia, Zebrina, Chlorophytum, Fern nephrolepsis – Boston fern. Stephanotis, Roseta (pale pink Rose), Bride Gladioli, Large white Gladioli.

Wire the foliages first. The Chlorophytum is wired as a Carnation grass and mounted on a 22 swg × 10". All the wires must be guttared. The Tradescantia is a firm foliage but it is a good idea to support the main stem with a silver wire before mounting onto a 22 swg × 10". Make sure the materials have been well conditioned.

Wire the flowers as bouquet work, using 32 swg binding wire. Make two curving tails using Stephanotis and Geranium. Make one shorter than the other. One curves to the left and to the right. Then make the centre tail. Attach the binding wire approximately 10″ from the tip of the fern. Gradually build out on the sides and up to the centre. Make the tail approximately 15″. Bend the wires down to form the handle.

Bind in the two curved tails of Stephanotis and Geranium. Keep the binding wire in one place. The top of the bouquet is made next. Hold the bouquet facing you and put in the height approximately half the length of the centre tail, using a fine-pointed piece of material. This piece leans slightly back to help with the balance of the bouquet. The width is gained by looking at the widest point in the curved sprays and bringing out the pieces a little longer.

Keep the small, dainty materials to the outline and the heavier materials to the centre. The touches of pink have been kept to the middle. Group the Roses. Fill in the outline and then the centre of the bouquet can be filled in. The material radiates from the centre. Look around the side of the bouquet and check it is not looking flat. When the bouquet is complete cut the handle and finish as usual.

VICTORIAN POSY   The posy materials are: Roseta, Sedum spectabile (green before changing to pink), Tweedia, pink Statice, Brodiaea, white Stock, pink Carnation.

Cut the Rose stem short, approximately ¾″ under the seed box. Pierce a 22 swg × 7″ or 10″ up the inside of the stem to the base of the head. Secure with a 32 swg silver wire. Gutta.

The other flowers are wired on 32 swg double leg mounts. The first 3 rows are left like that. No gutta is needed. The other flowers may need more support. Here I used a 26 swg × 7″ and pierced a wire up the stem on one Brodiaea and twisted another along side. The Stock needs each flower-head supported.

The pleated Carnation had a 24 swg × 7″ pierced up one piece with the other twisted alongside. This helps to cut down on the binding wire when making up the posy.

Wiring for a Victorian posy: a rosebud, carnation petals and ribbon

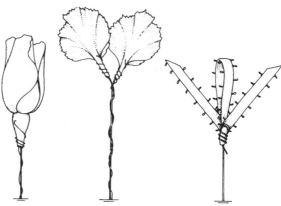

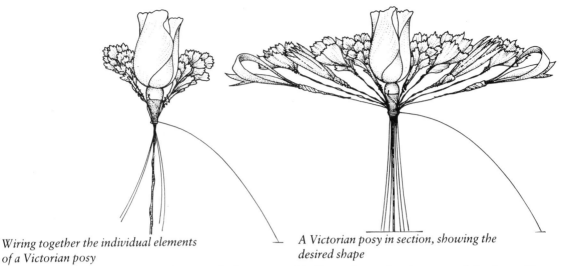

Wiring together the individual elements of a Victorian posy

A Victorian posy in section, showing the desired shape

To make, attach the 32 swg binding wire under the stem of the Rose. Keep the binding wire in one place. Start with the smallest flowers and grade the materials out. Work out the rows and check the colours before you start. Limit each row to one type of flower. Now place on the small leaves in reverse to hid the wires. Cut the wires to approximately 21–24″. Bind down. Gutta. The Carnation petals make a pleasing final row.

The ribbons can be wired on 26 swg × 7″ silver wire, with a simple leg mount. Gutta. Place these evenly around the posy. Place on the frill and check the size. Cut the handle to required length. Take off the frill. Cut round the scollops. Take the binding wire down to the bottom of the handle, and cut off. Gutta. Place the frill back on. Ribbon the handle as usual.

PARASOL The parasol is made up of: Hebe, blue Hydrangea, Cornflowers, cream Statice, Senecio Greyi.

Wire the material on 32 swg double leg mounts and gutta. Bind the flowers onto a guttared wire to form a garland and then sew them onto the parasol. If the parasol is going to be opened, small posies could be attached at the end of each spoke and a circlet round the top. The other idea is a garland of flowers made up on a string and sewn on round the edge of the parasol.

CORSAGE The corsage is composed of: Heather, Geranium leaves, Hosta. With the materials on 32 swg silver wire, double leg mounts. Gutta.

To make, choose a fine piece of Heather and a Hosta bud and attach the 36 swg binding wire approximately 2½–3″ from the tip of Heather. Grade the material and make the tail first. This is approximately 5″ in length. You can make it straight or curved. When the length is reached the binding wire stays in one place and a returned end is made. The longest point in the return end is approximately half the length of the tail. It does not want to appear flat and each flower should be seen clearly. Keep the spray light and dainty. Remember the spray should look as beautiful and delicate as a piece of jewellery.

Autumn wedding

Freesia straight spray
Red and yellow Freesia have been pipped to make this spray.

Chunky head-dress for a child bridesmaid
This head-dress includes: Euonymus, Hydrangea (bluey green), Achilea (yellow), Statice (peach-apricot), Chrysanthemum buds (bronze), yellow ribbons.

Crescent bouquet
The foliages used are: Euonymus, glycerined Beech, Begonia.
The flowers, in the same colours as for the head-dress, are: Hydrangea, Old Man's Beard, Statice, Achillea, Chrysanthemum, Clivia. This bouquet has been made as a small posy.

Winter wedding

Posy bouquet

The bouquet includes: Ivy leaves and berries, Cyclamen leaves, Camellia leaves, Helleborus foetidus, Helleborus Corsicus, Helleborus niger (Christmas Rose), Heather (white) and Hyacinth (white).

Head-dress

The materials for this head-dress are: Ivy leaves, Ivy berries, Heather, Hyacinth, Hellebores.

Curved mixed foliage corsage

This corsage, for the bride to wear going away, includes: Euonymus, Helleborus foetidus, Pittisporum, Ivy, Eleaegnus, Hebe and seedpods, Senecio greyii, Cassinia fulvida, Holly leaf osmanthus.

Winter wedding

POSY BOUQUET   Ivy leaves and Berries, Cyclamen leaves, Camellia leaves, Helleborus foetidus, Helleborus corsicus, Hellebore niger (Christmas Rose), Heather (white), Hyacinth (white).

Condition all the materials first – this is very very important. Wire the materials in order of lasting quality.

Ivy Leaves
Cut the stem to ¾–½". Wire with a 32 swg (0.28mm) silver wire. Single stitch. Double leg mount. Gutta.

Vary the size of the leaves. These are then sprayed up into twos and threes, the smallest leaf to the top of the wire, grading down to the largest. A 22 swg × 10" (0.71 × 260mm) is used. Gutta the leaves onto the wire. Try to make them look as much like the natural stem as possible. It is not necessary to gutta right to the bottom of the wire; approximately ½–¾" is plenty. Stand the made-up pieces in a pot so they do not get damaged.

Ivy Berries
Cut the stem to approximately ½". Use a 32 swg (0.28mm) silver wire. Take the wire across the top of the berry cluster and down to form a double leg mount. Pierce a 22 swg × 10" (0.71 × 260mm) wire up the stem and twist the silver wires round. Gutta.

Camellia
These leaves are very thick, firm and have a glossy texture. Use a 32 swg (0.28mm) silver wire. Make a small loop at the back and base of the leaf. Form a double leg mount. Pierce the 22 swg × 10" (0.71 × 260mm) into the stem and twist the silver wires around. Gutta. The smaller leaves can be mounted in twos.

Cyclamen
These leaves have an attractive shape and markings. Cut the stem to ¼–½". Make a simple stitch, double leg mount with 32 swg (0.28mm) silver wire. Pierce a 22 swg × 10" (0.71 × 260mm) wire up the stem and twist wires together. Gutta. Vary the size of the leaves, using five or seven.

Helleborus foetidus (The Stinking Hellebore)
Cut the stems short. Wire the heads with a 32 swg (0.28mm) silver wire. Double leg mount. Gutta. Carefully open the petals out to reveal the beautiful markings inside. Spray the flowers up in threes on 24 swg ×10". Grade the sizes down the wire.

Helleborus corsicus
These can be rather soft, so wire these last. Cut the stems to various lengths. The smallest flower has the longest stem, approximately 3–4". If possible, take the 22 swg (0.71mm) or 24 swg × 10" (0.56 × 260mm) up the inside of the stem. Secure the base of the stem with a 32 swg (0.28mm) silver wire. Gutta. You could wrap a little moist cotton wool round the base of the cut stem before covering with gutta.

Heather

Cut the stems to various lengths. Use a 32 swg (0.28mm) silver wire. Double leg mount. Support with a 24 swg × 10″ (0.56 × 260mm) and gutta.

Hyacinth

This is a favourite flower to use in wedding bouquets. Each bell is wired with a 32 swg (0.28mm) silver wire. Pierce the wire through the bulbous base of the bell and form a double leg mount. Gutta. If the pip or bell has no stem, use two silver wires. Take each one through to form a double leg mount in different directions. By twisting the wires together you form a stem. Spray the Hyacinths up in twos, threes and fives.

Stand the wired-up material in pots so you can see what you have to work with. Try to have a picture in your mind of how the bouquet will look before you start. If possible, have a full-length mirror in the workroom.

For the bouquet, you will need: 10 Christmas roses, 3 Corsicus, 3 Ivy Berry, 7 wires Helleborus foetidus, 9 wires Heath, 15 wires Hyacinth

Take seven wires which will form the outline to the bouquet. These should be pointed materials. Make sure the tops of the materials are all the same length. Attach the 32 swg (0.28mm) silver binding wire approximately 7″ down from the top. The binding wire stays in one place throughout the making of this bouquet. Bend the wires to form a circle. Two wires are bent down as a returned end. Two wires stay almost straight at the top and the other three wires help to make the circle on the sides. Place in a piece of Hyacinth to mark the centre – approximately ½–¾ of the outline length. This piece faces up towards the ceiling; it does not stick straight out following the line of the handle. Take the binding wire round each time to secure in the wires. Sometimes you can hold two to three pieces in and then bind. This helps to keep the bouquet light to hold. The handle comes straight down at the bottom of the bouquet. The back is kept flat on this posy.

Place a few large leaves round the centre – this helps to fill in and it draws your eye in towards the middle of the bouquet. Next, start to fill in around the outline edge, with nothing longer than the outline points. Think about the position of the materials and whether grouping the flowers is necessary. Look at the bouquet from different angles. Hold the bouquet in your left hand and bind with your right. Keep the bouquet away from your body so the flowers do not get damaged. Vary all the lengths: the small, pale and dainty materials help to make the outline points; the large, dark and heavier materials give the centre. Do not cross the wires; put them in where you wish them to remain. Do not bind on natural stems. The wires all radiate from the centre Hyacinth.

It is a good idea to look in a mirror during the making of the bouquet and also to hold the bouquet in the position it will be held. I look down on the top; you can then see if the bouquet looks flat on the sides. Make sure that the balance of the bouquet is correct; the weight needs to go to the back.

To finish the bouquet, wire three leaves with 32 swg (0.28mm) silver wire, double leg mount and gutta. Bind the leaves in. Make sure the good side is facing out. The loop is to the back of the bouquet. Hold the bouquet handle in your left hand with a clenched fist then cut the wires straight across ½–1″

under the hand. Taper the wires up the handle if necessary and make sure the handle is smooth. Take the binding wire down the handle. Slip the silver wire in between the stub wires, secure and cut off. Gutta the handle. Then finish with a ribbon and bow to the back of the bouquet. To ribbon the bouquet handle, choose a colour to match the bouquet flowers. Approximately 11–12 yds of 1″ ribbon with a non-slip surface will be needed.

Hold the bouquet in your left hand. Place 2″ of ribbon behind the handle, bring down and up the front of the handle. The shiny side of the ribbon is to the outside. Secure with a spray pin at the bottom. Now bind as a finger bandage catching in the width of the ribbon at the base. Bind at an angle up to the top of the handle making a loop and a slip knot at the top. Secure this with a bow.

HEAD-DRESS   Check the measurement of head first.

A guide
Frame: Four 22 swg × 12″ wires (0.71 × 310mm); overlap two 22 swg × 12″ (0.71 × 310mm) wires. Starting at the overlap bind the wires together with a 36 swg (0.20mm) binding wire. Work down to the end of the wires and then back to the other end. Cut off binding wire and gutta. Take the frame round a bucket or pot to help form a circle, overlap approximately 1–2″. Secure together with 36 swg (0.20mm) binding wire. Gutta over binding. Check the round shape.

Wire materials next, in order of lasting quality. Ivy leaves, Ivy berries, Heather, Hyacinth and Hellebores. All the materials are wired with a 32 swg (0.28mm) silver wire. Double leg mount. Gutta a little of the wire. Keep the materials in groups on the table then you can see amounts to work with.

If you are a right-handed person, hold the frame in your left hand and bind with the right. Attach the 36 swg (0.20mm) binding wire to the frame. The materials are bound on along the side of the frame. The first few pieces determine the width of the band. Approximately 1½″. The flowers and leaves are grouped through from side to side to form a pattern. Take the silver wire round the frame at an angle. Bind the materials underneath the natural stem and cut away unwanted wires from the double legs. This will keep the head-dress neat and light. Make sure the wires are cut away clearly so that there are no spiteful ends. It is a good idea for the head-dress to match the bouquet. Each piece of material is placed on close to or overlapping the piece that went in front. This head-dress has a full look to it. Make sure the pieces come well down on the sides of the frame so that the head-dress sits comfortably.

Keep working round the frame until the beginning is reached. Lift the first couple of pieces and continue to work right to the end of the frame. Secure the binding wire between last wires and frame. Cut off. Gutta over the last section. Push the flowers and leaves down so you cannot notice the finish. Check the positioning of the materials and then spray gently with water. Do not over-soak the Hyacinth otherwise they could go transparent.

CURVED MIXED FOLIAGE CORSAGE For the bride to wear going away.

Materials: You will need: Euonymus, Helleborus foetidus, Pittosporum, Ivy, Eleaegnus, Hebe and seedpods, Senecio Greyi, Cassinia fulvida, Holly leaf Osmanthus.

The materials are wired with a 32 swg (0.28mm) silver wire. Most of the leaves have a single stitch. Double leg mount, but the Osmanthus is very firm and only a loop at the base of the foliage is needed, then a double leg mount. The Hebe and Cassinia have the stems cut short and a loop at the base of material to support and a double leg mount.

Vary the sizes of the leaves as you wire them – it helps with the make-up of the corsage. Gutta all the wires starting just on the stem of the material. This will help to keep the moisture in the foliage so it will last longer. It is the shape, colour and texture that makes this corsage interesting.

Take a 36 swg (0.20mm) binding wire, choose a small pointed leaf and attach the binding wire approximately 3″ from the tip down the false leg. Place another leaf in slightly shorter on the left-hand side. This spray curves from left to right. Gradually build out on the left and tuck small pieces in on the right. Gradually build up in the middle towards the centre.

The materials must be graded through the spray. Take the binding wire at an angle down the tail part adding in the leaves as you go. Do not bind on the stems of the natural materials. The binding wire travels approximately 2–3″ according to the size of corsage being made. The binding wire then remains in one place and this is where the widest point should be in the spray.

The returned end can now be made. Place a small leaf in to form the longest point in the back so you can see the curve. Place in the outline materials first, do not let it get too solid. Next place in the centre looking at the build up in the tail and then work the materials around it. Vary the lengths. Make sure you bend the wires well and bind on the bend otherwise the binding wire and the materials will slip.

Turn the corsage round and look at how it will be worn. When the spray is complete, cut the wires under the longest leaf (approximately 1½″) and taper the stem. Take the binding wire down to the end. Cut away. Cover the false stem with gutta. If several leaves of one type of material are being used, group the leaves through the spray. The most colourful or dominate leaves should curve with the spray.

Moving large arrangements from church to reception

There will be a time when you will be asked whether you can move the flowers from the church after the service and set them up at the reception. My immediate answer would be 'no' and I will tell you why.

Large groups are arranged to look correct in their setting – once the background changes the whole effect will change. They never move properly, usually because your van is not large enough. You will often find the greatest difficulty getting through the traffic, and then working at the reception when they are just finalising all the food will be most difficult. We have done it on occasions and each time there have been more problems.

If you attempt to do it and the flowers at the end are not really looking good because you just have not had the time to do it properly, they are no credit to you. Remember, people seeing the flowers will not realise that you have struggled from the church with them. The whole idea is that they should not realise what has happened. If the flowers appear second-rate, they will just think that you have not done so well.

If time allows for the church groups to be properly stripped and then completely done again at the reception then the switch can be achieved properly and all should be well. A quick move, in the hope that all will go smoothly, is not for me. In the end, it will inevitably result in disappointment.

Party and wedding breakfast table-cloths

So often the whole beauty of the setting is spoilt by the poor quality of the table-cloths. We never seem to use round table-cloths on round tables or break away from the white cloth. In America so much effort goes into this area – coloured cloths, napkins and candles; all go to make the overall picture. There is nothing that takes away from the beauty of flowers more than a white table-cloth.

I was doing the flowers for the television programme 'Upstairs, Downstairs'. We had set up our flowers (pink Carnations and Fern) on the dinner table, which was beautifully laid out with superb glass, china and silver for something like fourteen guests when the director came in and said, 'that white table-cloth kills everything through the camera lens; it is ghastly'. So off everything came and a pale pink cloth was brought in. The difference it made was outstanding and something that has always backed my argument. Candles, napkins, china and linen should all be blended into the overall colour scheme.

The other point I mentioned is the use of round table-cloths. They look so much better on a round table, and the positioning of the square or oblong ones always take so much setting up.

Polished table-tops are wonderful surfaces on which to work and they reflect the beauty of the flowers but these are not often available. If you were to look under the cloth on many occasions, you would get a nasty shock. So often a disc of plywood or hardboard is used on top of a trestle or rough framework.

Wedding cake table decorations

A wedding cake standing on its own decorated table will be a focal point at any wedding breakfast. It also makes a very good background for photography and cutting the cake is one of those special moments everyone wants to record.

In the arrangement shown on the following pages, we have used a simple, round table covered with a cloth made from a blue lining material which has extra fullness around the table-top, pinched in at set points with bows of ribbon and garlanded along the table edge with fresh flowers and foliage. The garlanding is worked from the centre of the table-front edge outwards. Made on a piece of string cut to the correct length the flowers are of Helleborus foetidus, Hyacinth pips in blue, dark blue and white, Viburnum flowers, Ivy and small Viburnum leaves all mounted on double leg mounts of 32 swg silver wire (0.28mm). The pieces are held flat against the string parallel to the work top and carefully twisted just below the stalk twisting all the same way and working to a pattern. The correct length is made and pinned to the table edge.

The small bunches of flowers are made on special Oasis posy holders. They look like little plastic lettuce shakers with a piece of Oasis inside. The stems are just stuck into the wet Oasis, the Hyacinth are made up in small sprays of wired bells. Keep natural pieces of stems to add at the end making them look like little bunches.

When very small flowers are used, you can with difficulty secure these to the side of the table edge but the bunches do tend to fall forward all the time. To overcome this, the little Oasis holders may be fitted to a small bar of wood covered with ribbon, and this in turn is fixed at both ends to the table-cloth. The idea of these is excellent but the actual fixing leaves much to be desired and you must be so careful not to damage the table or fabric with pins or heavier fixing methods.

To make the cake-top each little flower has been wired. This gives lightness and enables the stems to be stuck into the oasis. The baby Ivy leaves and Hyacinth bells have been sprayed up. The container is a little piece of Coalport china in which we used to pot up our hand-made miniature Cyclamen. The top is 1″ across and it just holds a piece of Oasis 1 × 1″.

Wedding cake and table decorations

A wedding cake standing on its own decorated table will be a focal point at any wedding breakfast.

12. Flowers for Christmas

$\mathcal{T}$oday, with all the materials coming in from around the world, there is little chance of not being able to get what you require at Christmas. The flower shops will be full of materials.

After working for months with gum and glitter, and all the artificial materials, up to Christmas, I long for a few sprays of the yellow Winter Jasmine (*Jasminum nudiflorum*), some really small, dark green Ivy with venation markings made prominent from frosting, a little Mistletoe, tiny sprays of Tsuga with cones with a few real Christmas Roses and perhaps one or two green Orchids, with a stem or so of Chimonanthus fragrans. These all make up a wonderful low table centre. When I first started working with Constance Spry we had boxes of small, green Slipper Orchids coming in from the end of November, and these were so attractive and long-lasting. The other decoration would be a well-decorated Christmas tree, then a large pot of Hyacinths (Roman or Cynthellas) and a lovely Azalea would be extras.

Mixed reds always look good at Christmas and red Carnation in clove and scarlet, both perpetual-flowering and spray, are useful. Red Ranunculus and red Anemones are excellent but not easy to find. Roses are very expensive and except for Mercedes which is rather orange, not good because they soon go over and blue with age. Some red spray Chrysanthemum is very good. I prefer it to the large blooms; it seems a better colour. Use it with dark Holly plus berries.

White flowers are also good with variegated Holly, and look well arranged on a mirror base. Hyacinths, Freesia, Chrysanthemum, Carnations and paper white Narcissi would make a nice group with a grey Eucalyptus foliage. For a cream/green effect, you could add Poinsettia and creamy white Euphorbia, and cut down on the true white flowers. Yellows are easy; Chrysanthemum in different varieties would be all that you would need. Another small and appealing decoration is a small bowl of good Christmas Roses, a few small Hyacinths and a little Christmas tree foliage, plus Mistletoe. I associate Daffodil and Lilac with spring and do not want them over the Christmas period. The paper white Narcissi are available from early winter and are most attractive. Roman Hyacinths are another favourite of mine, but these at present are really difficult to obtain. Let's hope some grower finds a good stock and builds them up, because we do not want to loose them. A few years ago the paper white was nearly lost but it is now coming back. I believe a good strain has been introduced from the Middle East.

Although I don't choose it myself, you can introduce some silver, in the form of plastic leaves, to a real white flower arrangement. Some of the sprays of fern are very decorative and stood on a mirror base, or arranged in a silver or mirrored trough, and on a polished candlelit table, they can make a really charming decoration. This is when good glass comes into its own. White, silver and glass look so good together. Sprays of silver bells and also small silver baubles may be added to obtain a pretty effect for the festive season.

White Anemones, small spray Carnations and little white Chrysanthemums and perhaps for scent a few stems of white Freesia, would all go together giving interesting shapes and would not appear too heavy. The White Singapore Orchids are light, dainty and very elegant. Most important of all, these flowers I have mentioned will last through the Christmas period without too much attention. Keep the water table up and, when you can, the temperature down as low as possible. Change the air by opening the windows for a short period – it will help, especially if heavy smokers have been present for a time.

Preparing for Christmas

At Christmas time, people who normally do not attempt any floral decorating other than to stand a flowering pot plant in the window have a go and bring in flowers and foliages to their rooms to dress them up. In this section of the book I want to give you some ideas that I hope will help you with your decorations. None are difficult but some will take time to make.

The beauty of making Christmas decorations with artificial material is the fact that you can get well ahead early in the year. Paper flowers can be cut out and stored ready for assembling at a later date. Materials usually come into the shops by early September and certainly, if you are connected in the flower trade, your basic materials from abroad will have reached you during the late summer. The only problem is that the whole supplies do not come in together but, by building up your raw materials into groups, when all is collected you can progress straight away with assembling your decorations.

Decorations at Christmas time

Decorations for Christmas vary from plants to arrangements in fresh, dried and artificial materials. The seasonal ideas shown on page 128 are described on the following pages, complemented by other Christmas suggestions.

WALL DECORATION From the back right-hand side we have something in dried and fresh material which will hang on the wall. It is made on a piece of board 6 × 2″ on which moss had been firmly tied and then it is backed with a piece of plastic material. You could do this equally well with a piece of Oasis *Sec* glued to the back of cardboard or wood.

All the pieces of Holly, Ivy, Blue Pine, glycerined Beech and seed heads of Poppy are mounted on double leg-mounts, 22 × 7″ (90 × 180mm), and worked in to the mossed base which had some dried Hydrangea heads pinned onto it to help cover the green surface. Use your mounted pieces exactly as you would when doing an arrangement of cut flowers – bringing your pieces through in sweeps of different shapes and colours.

Ideas for the Christmas period

The nuts have been wired and mounted on more wire and, in some cases, they were just glued to the wire. This gives a different shape and colour. Use a gimlet to make holes through which to thread the wire, and a gauge of the correct thickness to hold the weight of the spray of nuts. Hang from a cord and add ribbon and bows to pick up the colouring.

FLORAL ARRANGEMENT The arrangement is of mixed red flowers with dark green and grey foliage and a green plastic bowl (typical of the flower trade) has been used to hold the flowers and foliage. The stems are secured into Oasis covered with a layer of 2″ netting which was secured to the bowl rim with Oasis tape. The foliage is of Holly, Eucalyptus, Ivy and Ivy berries and the flowers are Rose (Mercedes) which is an excellent, lasting variety of good shape and colour. Also incorporated are red Freesia, red spray Carnations and scarlet Carnations.

Owls on the branch are set in log with decorations. All the pieces of Christmas foliages with berries are made up into two clusters to balance. The bottom piece is now in the form of a table setting with candles attached but it is described more fully on page 131, as a wreath in use as a door decoration.

AZALEA PLANT This is stood in a pot-holder and the soil surface is covered with moss. This helps to keep the ball of soil moist all the time which is so important with the Azalea. It must never become dry otherwise the buds and leaves will drop. It is available in many shades of pink, red and white and also in two tones. At Christmas time, the red is very popular.

ARTIFICIALS ON A LOG This type of decoration always sells well. It was in the first instance thought out for a child's decoration but we have made many of this type and it seems to be appreciated by all ages. It is simple to make and will use up the small oddments of material that always accumulate over a period of time. There are no set colour schemes but I find that the natural-looking foliages in mixed greens with the addition of reds and orange berries look best. Silver, white, gold and glittered material is not really suitable for this type of decoration.

First choose your log – something with an interesting outline that sits firmly on the ground. It may be necessary to shave a strip off the base to get it sitting comfortably. You may leave it like this or set it on a cork mat. If there is any chance of it scratching the furniture, glue pads of felt to the 'pressure points'.

Decide on the placing of your foliages – one, two or on a large log perhaps three clusters. If you are adding some 'wild life' decide where the branch should be placed and drill out a hole to hold it. This just adds height and interest.

The position of each foliage cluster should be marked with a couple of 1½″ nails. This work may be done in advance of doing the decorating so that once ready to start it is a straight forward production line adding the foliage plus branch.

Another job that may be done is to sort out all the oddments of foliage and wire them up on double leg 22 swg × 7″ mounts. Those pieces on long natural stems may well stick into the holder without wiring but short bits should be on 'legs'.

The making up is as follows. Add small lumps (the size of a golf ball) of Dryhard or Plasticine to the nails and press well down. Into this stick your pieces of foliage, getting a variation of lengths and interesting shapes next to each other so they all show up well. Arrange as you would a posy of mixed greens. See that the stems radiate well and that the holding material does not show. Gradually this will dry out and the pieces will be held firm. Attach the branch at the last moment before displaying.

PYRAMID TREE IN A POT
2 Oasis *Sec* cones
1 thin flower cane
flower pot to fit in china pot cover
sand
Sphagnum Moss
32 swg reel wire and string
Lichen moss
Pins 22 swg × 7" (0.71 × 180mm). Cut in ½ then bend
Artificial plastic pine
Pine cones
22 swg × 7" (0.71 × 180mm) wire for double leg mount
Red and gold balls on wires – gutta with percha and then crinkle paper
Parcels – dry foam, crinkle paper, ribbon

Take the flower pot and cover the holes with a small piece of paper or plastic. Fill with damp sand. Make sure it will fit in an attractive pot cover. Cut the top off one of the Oasis cones. Push the cane up through centre of cut-off cone and then secure the other one on top so it looks like a pyramid. Push the cane into the sand.

Tease the Sphagnum Moss, removing any unwanted material, such as twigs and stones. Make sure the moss is damp as it is easier to work with. It will soon dry out and help to hold materials in place. Take a handful of moss and lightly cover the tip of the cone, secure in place with 32 swg silver wire (0.28mm) or string. Gradually work down and round the cone, only cover sparingly otherwise it will be difficult to get wires and stems through.

Place the flower pot in the pot cover, this will help with the proportion of the tree being made. Cut the pine, if needed, with wire cutters. Place a small piece in at the top of the cone and then pieces around the base so you can see the size. You will gradually build out to the bottom. Vary the lengths of the pieces and try to think of how a Conifer grows. The pieces want to go in at an angle not sticking straight out. Turn the tree all the time. Do not work in one area.

Once you have an attractive shape with some spaces, pin on the Lichen Moss with 22 swg × 7" (0.71 × 180mm) wires cut in half and bent to make a hairpin. The moss must be soaked for a little while before use then it can be spread out more easily but remember it wants to show.

The Pine cones can be wired with 22 swf × 7" (0.71 × 180mm) wires. These can be guttared for a neater finish. To wire the Pine cones take the wire round the base of the Cone in between the scale like pieces and then twist the wires together.

The little balls can be purchased on wires. Gutta these with gutta percha and then coloured crepe or gold crinkle paper. Spray the balls up in twos and threes

– they look more effective grouped together rather than used singly.

The little parcels are made with small pieces of foam. This is light and can easily be attached to the tree with a guttared wire.

Fairy lights could be pinned round the tree after the Sphagnum Moss and then the cable in between the lights can be covered quite easily. Take care not to puncture the electric wire.

COFFEE TABLE CENTRE PIECE
Wooden dish
Various cones and Lotus seed pods
Piece of Dryfoam, wire netting, Oasis tape
Lichen Moss
2 Robins
Velvet ribbon (rust colour)
Plastic Spruce

Choose a suitable container for this arrangement. Place a piece of foam in the centre of the dish and cover it with a piece of wire netting. Now you can secure this down with the Oasis tape.

Cover the foam with a light covering of Lichen Moss. Remember to soak this first – it then feels more like a sponge and is easier to work with. Use 22 swg × 7″ (0.71 × 180mm) hairpins to secure the Moss. Wire the cones with a 22 swg × 10″ or 7″ wire (0.71 × 180mm). Some cones may be on natural branches so you can use them in this way.

Use a large cone in the centre and then place a few cones and pieces of Spruce round the edge of the container to give the size and shape. Continue to turn the container grouping the materials from one side to the other or you can use the cones in varieties to give more impact. The Spruce and Lichen Moss can be used in between the cones.

The robins add a festive touch to the arrangement and the velvet ribbon picks up the colour of the birds' breasts. The ribbon is wired on a 22 swg × 10″ (0.71 × 260mm) double leg mount, and guttared.

Christmas door rings

The two rings, as shown on page 133, are made up on mossed 8″ and 10″ frames, backed with polythene to stop any dampness marking the paintwork. The foliage has all been wired on 22 swg × 7″ (71 × 180mm). They are made up of green and variegated Holly, Pine, Ivy with berries, pine cones, Cupressus, Lichen moss with small artificial fruits and berries. They are hanging from a 1½″ velvet ribbon which has been pinned into the top of the door where no marks will show; the two types of ribbon used to make the bows and the ends link up with the materials on the wreath surface.

To follow this idea through, if space permits, one could have the rings hanging from the ceiling set in two tiers with ribbons and bows coming down to three or four points on each ring.

Another way to use a ring of this kind is as a table centre, similar to an advent ring. Tall candles are set in candle holders well up above the foliage. The candle holders I believe to be an excellent idea: they do hold the candle firmly and give it an extra 1″ to burn down which helps from the safety angle.

Fresh fruit with artificial foliages

This is a dual-purpose decoration for Christmas when you have so much about that it is difficult to find room for everything on display. The fruit may be removed for eating and easily replaced with more so as to keep your decoration.

The group is set in an old copper pan – an excellent container for this type of decoration because it has a wide top and it is easy to arrange the fruit. In the base is dry Oasis (Oasis Sec), covered over with a layer of wire netting leaving a large hole centre-back for the electric candle (see also page 135). This I made from a cardboard covered with red velvet. A lamp holder is held in the top with the candle bulb and it is plugged in to the nearest power supply

Arrange the foliage – plastic and metallic fronds, even some home-made leaves from crinkle paper, sprayed up into fronds.

the pineapple is set up on a sharp cane stuck into the basal centre core. The grapes are wired and hooked onto the netting to allow them to flower over the front edge. The other fruits are just piled up on the flat base of netting which helps hold them. Any not remaining firm may be held by placing a small cocktail stick into the base. Do not puncture more than is really necessary because once damaged they do not keep so well.

Christmas decoration for the door

This door with its inlaid panels to match the wallpaper has been decorated for a party. It is in places such as this that extra decorations can be used and they do not take up valuable space.

Candles and lights

Any decoration is more attractive when well lit, be it by a spotlight from above or by lighting incorporated into the arrangment. At Christmas the use of lights on trees and in special arrangements adds to the atmosphere. The use of real candles on Christmas trees has gone, thank goodness, because these were a real fire hazard. Recently we have received very good, realistic white candles with electric flames from abroad. These easily clip on the tree branches and, although inclined to be bulky, are most effective. One special point to remember is that the candles must be upright so that they imitate the real thing convincingly.

The problem that I find difficult to solve is how to get rid of the electric wires. This is a must because a most attractive tree can be spoilt by a maze of wires. Always make sure you get the green wired sets. I prefer all white lights, but you can get sets of self-coloured or mixed colours, and for certain decorations these can look excellent.

When wiring a tree, start at the tip of the branch and bring the wire down as far as possible on the underside of the branch. Tighten each bulb as you work out the placement of each light. Secure with small pieces of guttared wire, as fine silver wire may cut the rubber/plastic flex surface. Try to spread the bulbs evenly. If you are using more than one set of lights, work to sections, making it easier to keep the wires hidden, rather than going all over the area. Always check your light circuit before attaching to the tree.

Finish off low down at the back of the tree with your final light so that all units of wire can be joined to one junction box out of sight.

Candle holder

Often I am very critical about additional items used as decorations and tend to dismiss them as gimmicks. The plastic candle holder is an exception. This is an excellent addition to the necessary equipment for the flower arranger and for once it is something that is cheap to buy. It will give an extra 1–2″ to any normal-sized candle and this in itself saves money because candles are expensive, especially if you want the special colours which so often are not produced in the elegant length of 12–15″. The 8–10″ candles are too short for fair sized decorations. By placing your candle in a plastic holder, you can lift it and give at least one more inch of burning time with safety.

They are fixed into the Oasis by pressing the tapered key to the base of the holder into the soaked Oasis. They are very stable and this is another point in their favour. Sometimes candles placed straight into Oasis tend to rock about. They are simply designed and I doubt whether you would really know they were being used without really looking into the flowers.

A while ago, there were some on the market in aluminium with a serrated rim to the base which was supposed to cut into moss and bark, but I found these rather poor quality. The plastic ones, designed only for use with Oasis, are excellent. You could also make a hole in your cork bark and then secure them to the bark surface with glue. Glue is an important item for today's florist.

Single electric candle

For a pleasing effect, you can make a large electric candle to stand within an arrangement of fruit and foliages on a sideboard.

You will need a stiff, cardboard cylinder holder about 1½–2″ in diameter and 15–18″ high. Cover this with a good quality red, or some other suitable coloured, velvet. Once covered, fix a collar to the top of the candle to hold the bayonet socket light fitting and a small amount of conduit. The electric bulb should fit in the top of the velvet-covered tube, but not quite close enough to burn it. The wire is threaded through the stem of the candle and out just near the base of the tube. Again, when using, do get the candle upright and the lead going out at the back. You may need an extra piece of netting to support the candle.

Arrange the fruits and foliage in the normal way around the base of the candle. This makes a very pleasing centre-piece for a buffet and can be used any time during the year.

Tsuga canadensis

This is one of the most useful of the conifers. It makes a very pretty-shaped tree and the branches when cut are long-lasting and appear as a light foliage. So many conifers seem heavy and can only be used in the winter period with large flowers and other foliages. The Tsuga can be used all the year. The back of the stems are a light grey colour and it is often used reversed to give a pleasing effect. The weeping branches carry attractive little cones which at Christmas time can be lightly frosted to give a most charming effect. I feel that, except for the true Christmas tree and Blue Cedar, this is my favourite evergreen 'conifer' for cutting and I would always make room for one in the garden.

Tinsel candle

This can make a good centre to the candlestick and a change from the wax candle. A tinsel candle is quite easy to make. You will require a length of dowelling, 12–14″ long, and a good, tapered shape. The candle should be at its thickest about 1″ from the base. Bind it tightly. Now cut some red/orange tin foil to make a flame, in small leaf-shape pieces with a wire at their back and finely-cut edges. Bind these on at the tip of the candle and then when bound in, shape up and twist to give a flame shape. Then cover with white crepe paper, about ½″ wide. Get a good shape to your candle base. On to this frame bind your tinsel. The tinsel will go on easily, if twisted carefully to keep an even thickness. Secure at the base with Sellotape.

Fireplace

To decorate a fireplace for Christmas is fun. It adds to the attraction of the room, is an excellent way to show anything really well because this is a focal point in the room. Another point in its favour is that the warmth of the fire gives off the pine smell into the room.

First assess where the swags can be hung safely because as they become dry so the fire hazard can increase. Remember that they must be really secure and in no way should the fixing deface the wood or brick work. They are heavy when fresh, so will need a really firm fixing. Measure carefully the amount of swagging needed and get all the shapes carefully worked out.

The first part of the construction is to get the wire netting frame made – two wire layers with packed damp moss between them. Firm even packing is important, getting fullness to the shape so that they do not appear flat. Wire up or string the edges and if necessary secure a rod or cane along the top hanging edge for strength. Cover the back with plastic sheeting – this keeps the moisture in and protects the wall or furnishings from the back layer. Cover the front with tissue paper. This keeps your hands clean and free from moss and mud which tends to stick to you. Select your foliage pieces and pin on a flat layer of cupressus first to make a base cover. Done with hair pins of 22 swg × 3½" (0.71 × 90mm). Now select the different types of foliage you are using – these are on double leg mounts and usually on 22 swg × 7" (0.71 × 180mm) wire. Work from one end of your frame to the other. In other words, the front pieces under the mantelshelf were all going to the centre bow. This gives a neat start on the outside edge and the more difficult part at the centre is under the ribbon. The side drops were done in the same way, but could have been worked from the centre if extra fullness and shaping were needed there.

The 'flowers' on the left-hand side are, in fact, just branches with lichen or Larch cones attached (natural branches, not man-made) with some leaves of Mahonia Bealei as a focal point. These are arranged in a copper trough – used to link up with the setting which calls for warm homely equipment. The old copper coal scuttle would make another suitable container at some time – perhaps filled with mixed flowers from the herbaceous border in the summer.

Christmas fireplace

Christmas decorations

The following may be presented in a planted bowl or flat oblong basket:

MIXED REDS	*GREEN/WHITE*
Azalea	Azalea
Red Kalenchoe	Hyacinth
Cyclamen	Cyclamen
Polyanthus	Lily of the Valley
Poinsettia	Cream Poinsettia
Red Chrysanthemum	Polyanthus

A well-planted bowl or low, flat basket is a wonderful Christmas decoration. This can be on-going for a few months if the correct materials are chosen. The foliage plants should last well; the bulbous plants will have to be replaced with other plants as the flowers go over, but the bulbs can be kept for later planting in the garden.

When using a basket, try to find a lining, such as a plastic tray, that will fit it; otherwise you can use a layer of thick polythene, provided care is taken not to puncture it. However, just as a safety measure, it is always wise to stand any planted bowl or basket on a cork mat to check any marking on polished surfaces from condensation or scratching.

Choose your plants carefully and see that they have had a good drink before knocking them out of the pots ready for planting. If using a good plant compost there will be no need for drainage; just put a little gravel then a good layer of the soil into the base of the container. Now place out the plants to give different heights, interesting leaf shapes and colours next to each other, and place the low, flowing materials over the front. Depending on the size of the container you will need anything from five different subjects upwards to a dozen in a fairly large basket.

Do not overcrowd; allow each subject to be clearly seen. Usually they are planted as a facing arrangement but with a pleasing and clever selection of plants which are fairly low, you can make an excellent table centre by introducing interesting mosses, bark, and small pieces of rock and gravel. You will get different shapes and colours which all help to make a really good decoration. Do not make the soil too deep. Having watered the ball of soil around the plant roots, you can carefully spread out the root system so that nothing is damaged and the plant will not need such a depth of soil to hold it firm. The soil really only holds moisture and plant food, and keeps the plant firm and in an upright position. You can still supply its needs by changing the root layout.

Once placed in position, firm round with the prepared compost. John Innes Potting Compost 1 or 2 will be excellent. Do not use garden soil unless it is in really excellent condition and free from weed seeds. Ninety-five per cent of garden soil would be unusable. Any large pieces of stone should now be placed in position, and then fill in around the plants with the compost, firming carefully so that you do not damage the root systems. The soil should come about ¼–½" below the rim. Place on the bark, gravel, sand and moss in

A Christmas cake top arrangement, in a silver egg-cup or small goblet

A Christmas cake garland for the base of the cake, matching the elements used in the cake top decoration

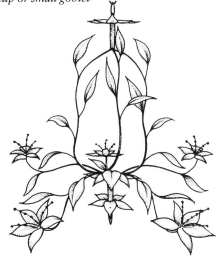

A paper floral chandelier: crinkle paper leaves are wired and bound to make this elegant shape, and 'pearls' are used for the centre of the flowers.

A facing arrangement for Christmas; baubles are wired up with artificial Christmas decorations and bare twigs of larch

interesting positions, keeping the colours of the foliage against a good background. Water lightly with a fine rose to settle the soil and help firm it.

Remember there is no free drainage so do not over-water, just keep the foliage free from dust by lightly spraying overhead. Bear in mind the different requirements of each plant and keep the base just moist. The addition of a little charcoal will keep the soil sweet. Over-watering can quickly turn your plant foliage yellow and spoil the whole arrangement. Plants requiring drier conditions should be grouped together. As the foliage plants grow, stake and tie them in to keep them tidy and within bounds. As flower arrangers know, any bits removed can be used in the next bouquet or decoration.

Old-fashioned garden wreaths

These two funeral wreaths were produced by two members of my staff, Philippa Eve and Helen Woodcock. Two designs, one done on an Oasis frame with garden flowers worked as a 'tapestry', so loved by Constance Spry, and the other of five clusters of herbs on a mossed, wire base lightly covered first with Bay leaves. Both show the use of garden materials simply worked into set patterns. Look carefully at the detail – they are both excellent pieces of work using interesting materials which are all simple to grow. (These illustrate another reason why the florist should have some back-up from local garden supplies.) The following have been used:

Clematis, Fairy (Floribunda Rose), Cecille Brunner, Polygonum, Hebe, Euonymus, Cornflower, Hydrangea, Hedera, Eryngium, Dianthus, Heather, Gypsophilla, Astrantia, Bun Moss, Senecio Greyi, Geranium leaves, Lilliput Zinnia, Sedum, Bay. Rue, Mint, Purple Sage, Mace.

13. Funeral flowers

$\mathcal{A}$lthough changes have taken place during the last few years, many people still feel that flowers in one form or another should be present at funerals. A great deal has been said and written in the press and some consider that all monies which would have been spent on flowers should go instead to charities; but I still feel the need for flowers both arranged in the church and more to accompany the coffin to the grave. I believe that Interflora were correct when they put out some time ago the statement, 'what words can't adequately express, flowers can'.

Today cremations are now more frequently the final stage in the life-cycle, yet still this service may be accompanied by beautiful floral tributes both in the form of flower arrangements in the crematorium and simple made-up work which may be passed on to old people's homes as decorations for the residents after the service.

I maintain that funeral flowers can be just as beautiful as any bouquet, and every thought and care should go into making the tributes so that it is right for the person and the occasion.

Wreath work

A great deal of thought should be put into the floral tribute. Take, for instance, an order for an old gardener. Here is the occasion when a wreath of mixed garden flowers and foliages may be used. A loose wreath, combining as many flower shapes and colours as can be found at the time, would be ideal. The frame may be lightly mossed and greened then a 'tapestry' of colour added. For this an Oasis wreath frame will be very easy to use. Another suitable style could be made from clusters or groups of interesting, mixed foliage or something such as small tips of Bay or Portuguese Laurel. This shows a real expression of feeling for the deceased.

It is important that the florist gets access to interesting foliages and flowers. Nothing out of the ordinary can ever be produced from basic market produce. There are some people growing interesting materials and these are the ones to contact. It is interesting to me to go through a class of students, perhaps twelve to sixteen, all working on the same wreath frames but with different materials, from those basic commercial supplies to those collected entirely from our own garden. There is no doubt which makes the better wreath. You can look at all the workmanship, which will differ greatly as will the way the material has been handled, but the overall effect is always the best from the mixed herbs and the real garden flowers. At Constance Spry's we are spoilt by having such wonderful material but there are chances of getting some of these things from time to time and I don't believe that some of the florists today would see them in the right light.

Wreath work may be carried out in many shapes. I tend to favour the traditional designs, such as the wreath, chaplet, cross, posy pad and spray on a board. There are a few I would avoid, including the 'Gates of Heaven' and 'Vacant Chair'. However, it is the colouring, foliages and flowers which are used that make the wreath a success, or not. Carrying out the work on the very detailed frames is very time consuming and to do it well with the correct size of flowers makes it very costly. Remember the smaller the flower you use the better the shape will be and keeping to similar flower texture in its different colours will make for more even work than using many different flowers.

Anything done in Oasis is going to last longer (if it is watered properly) and needs less wiring. Furthermore it can, after the funeral, be sent to an old peoples' home to be used as a decoration, thereby putting it to another use which helps when explaining the cost to a prospective customer. So often they do not wish to pay for something they feel will be a waste of money.

An important point to remember when making funeral pieces is that you should not moss too thickly; it should be just firm enough to hold the wire mounts but not to make the flowers and foliages appear to stand on a ridge up well above the ground-level. This is one of my chief complaints about the frames held in the plastic holders. They are excellent for holding the Oasis in a tray of moisture but far too deep and out of proportion, especially with the smaller frames. When using an extra lump of moss it needs to be about the size of half a tennis ball, not a great mound, to hold the spray. Flowers should be carefully chosen, wired accordingly to their needs and placed well so that the overall effect looks balanced.

Herb wreath

1)   A standard 10″ wreath frame is mossed with no fullness. It is important to keep it round and even in firmness and not too thick.

2)   It is lightly covered with Bay leaves. Cut ⅓ off the bottom of each leaf and wipe over with tissue paper, to clean. Pin the Bay leaves on with 22 swg × 10″ cut into 2″ hairpins, two pins per leaf. No pins must be showing, therefore they should not be placed more than ⅓ of the way up the main vein of the leaf.

3)   Divide the frame into sections, using wires, with the top of the wire bent over.

4)   Split the herbs into 5 sections, using wires, with the top of the wire bent over.

5)   Double leg mounted with 22 swg × 7″ and positioned on the frame in round clusters, varying the length of the pieces in order to cover the whole of the frame. We placed herbs of the same colour or shade opposite one another.

6)   Check the back for any mounts in case they have come through the moss.

7)   Spray to keep fresh.

Garden wreath

1)   For this piece of floristry an 8″ Oasis wreath frame was used. First it is soaked in water for 20 minutes.

2)   It is based with Bun Moss, Hydrangea, Ivy leaves and Reindeer Moss, by pinning on the frame with 22 swg × 2″ hairpins.

3)   Determine the height and width at which to make the wreath, the height being approximately the width of the frame.

4)   First arrange the varying pieces around the base, making sure we cover the plastic around the base of the frame. The inner edge must be kept short in order to keep the inside free, keeping the round shape of the frame.

5)   Put in the central row to establish the height over the whole of the frame.

6)   Build up from the outer rows to the centre, making sure the pieces are of varying length and depth.

7)   Pieces were not kept in set groups or colours, but keeping the recessive colours low down, and the lighter more delicate pieces up over the top.

8)   Dampen with fine spray of water to keep fresh.

Mark out the various points on the frame for each group and look at it carefully from above. Certain flowers appear to take up more room than others. Foundation work should be pinned or secured in some way onto the surface, which is first covered with tissue paper. This keeps the white and pale material from getting discoloured and stops the moss or base showing through. Always bring the flowers right down onto the edge of the frame and get them overlapping evenly and close together. As they dry out they will shrivel slightly and then the gaps appear, so keep them moist and covered with damp paper as you work. They should be secured to the frame in a clockwise manner. If working on a cushion frame, work from the corners to the point where the spray is secured which should be in the top left section. Always leave the area under the spray until last in case your pieces run out. You can fill the gap there with a leaf.

Always back the mossed frame with Laurel leaves or some form of wreath wrap but don't stop the moss acting as a sponge for the flower stems. These should be down into the moss on the top surface. See that no wires come through the back of the frame which makes them difficult to handle. Both these last points, of course, do not apply when using the Oasis-type frames.

I know today it is becoming more difficult to obtain the different frames for wreath work and this situation I understand will not improve – in fact I am told the wire frames are gradually on the way out. This to me is a retrograde step; the best funeral work without doubt is still produced on the mossed frame, and while I am connected with floristry there will always be work done on wire frames in our training school. I can see the reason for the modern bases; they have their advantages and are very useful. But they are too thick and bulky-looking to give the really balanced result in many cases. The bigger frames give the better results.

Chrysanthemums with garrya elliptica

A hamper basket has been chosen to hold sprays of Ayr Chrysanthemums in three colours and red Chrysanthemum blooms. The foliage is Garrya elliptica in a fairly advanced stage of flowering, the flower tassels being over 5" long on some stems due to the very early season.

14. A demonstration of floristry

I am often asked by students how they can start demonstrating. It is not an easy question to answer. I always say, start in a small way and make a name for yourself. Once known you will find the bookings come in. Be yourself; do not conform to a set type, but be able to adjust to the audience.

I know that some organisations stipulate that you have to be trained by them to be able to demonstrate. I believe that this is wrong. You will get a much better and wider approach to the subject from somebody not controlled by any rules.

There is more to doing a demonstration than many people would think and it needs planning with care. A lot will depend on the audience – you may be doing it for a group of girls from a Young Farmers Club, or for the members of the local Church – so you must choose your title for your talk accordingly. If already given, still gear it to the correct level and topic. Some clubs are very well-organised and powerful in the flower world, and expect a very high standard, although often I feel perhaps a down-to-earth, basic demonstration may do no harm.

In many cases when invited to talk, you are given a subject or title. If not, I believe in using a simple title and giving it as wide a coverage as I can in the given time. From choice I think about one-and-a-half hours is plenty of time to cover your topic and hold the interest of the audience. Some people go on for two hours but this can be too long. On the other hand, when asked to do half-an-hour as an after-lunch speaker, this does not give you time to get started. In this case, I would take a few things already done.

It is quite a good idea to have a few titles to offer as this makes it easier for the people who are booking you up. Such titles as 'Making the most of the early spring Flowers', 'Party Flowers', 'Flowers around the Home', 'Autumn colourings at their Best' and 'My Favourite Containers' are subjects giving plenty of scope.

I believe during the demonstration that you should do seven to nine arrangements, depending on size. According to instructions drawn up, some of these may be raffled at the end so be careful not to use materials that you cannot part with. People know that they cannot have the containers but do like if possible to take the arrangement intact in Oasis. This often makes it a problem for me because I do not use much Oasis, preferring always to work with wire netting. This is just a personal choice which I stick to whenever I can. In this case, always have paper in which to roll up the flowers.

Always arrive in good time to get set up before the audience comes in. You will find it difficult to work quietly if people are coming up and asking questions. Time given to setting out everything in order with careful placement of containers and flowers well out of sight makes for a slick presentation. If the table from which you are working is not covered, throw over a loose drape of something like green hessian. This immediately gives you an area under the table where you can stand your waste box and any of your packing boxes. Most clubs have their bench covered and also small tables on which to display your finished work already set up on the stage. Always check that the table is firm and will not rock about. It is most off-putting if things start to move when working.

I believe that it is good to work on a large dust sheet, so once your table is in position, lay this out behind it and then set up your buckets and flowers on it, leaving plenty of space to work. A small stool or chair at your right-hand side is ideal for standing your flowers on. As you work, you can take out the stems from the water and keep everything tidy. A piece of clear or black plastic should be placed on top of the table on which will stand the turntable. This will keep the table cover clean and dry. The turntable will be a great asset – you should slowly turn it so that everyone has a chance to see what you are doing. Do have this at the correct height for working comfortably.

All your equipment should be on your left-hand side – netting, pin holders, Oasis, vases, rubber bands, string, cocktail sticks, wire, Oasis tape, knife and vases that you will be using – so that everything you need is readily available. It does not look good if you have to disappear under the bench and go searching for a container or rummage in a black sack for bits and pieces. Everything should be slick and smooth-running. Remember, if you are attached to a microphone that you can only travel a certain distance. Be careful that you do not cut the lead or trip over it. The new radio microphones are much better and pick up your voice wherever you go. Place out on the bench your scissors and secateurs, plus a cloth to wipe up any surplus water. Now all should be ready. You should have a glass of water handy if you feel that you may need it.

You will be introduced – sometimes really well, sometimes leaving a lot to be desired. A good Chairman can work wonders. Over the years, I have heard some amazing statements – one of the best was probably when the lady introducing me got up and said 'next month we have ... but the tickets are already sold out so if you have not been lucky, please do not keep ringing up. At any rate, today we have Harold Piercy and he should give us an interesting afternoon.' Talk about second best!

Try and start with something topical or amusing. Get them interested in what you are saying, then start the first arrangement. You can never go wrong by showing how to cut and use wire netting. Place it in your container. Tie it in and generally promote wire netting as the best flower holder. Some people will find Oasis is easier to use; it does hold flowers where you put them so it may be as well to do one or two in this. Oasis is now in different strengths so by choosing the right one, you should have no problem. Talk your way through it. Then say what you are going to use in your arrangement. List the foliage first then the flowers, giving an approximate number of stems. Say where and how it would be placed. Three-quarter fill with water. Talk your way through your arrangement.

I would suggest that you point out that there are no rules but only guidelines

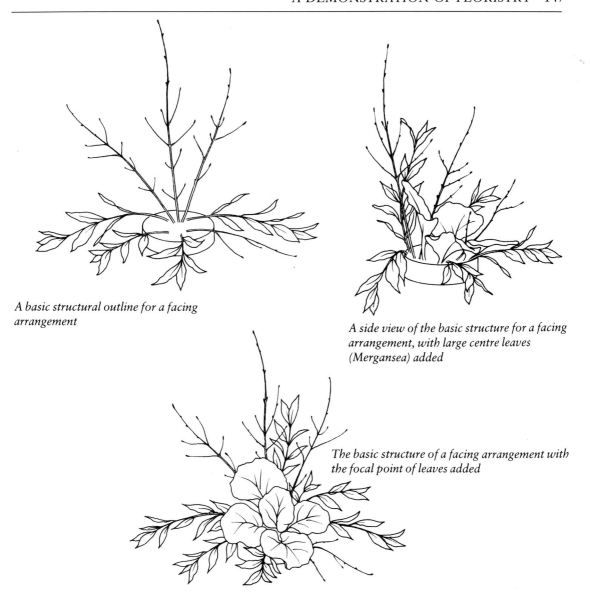

A basic structural outline for a facing arrangement

A side view of the basic structure for a facing arrangement, with large centre leaves (Mergansea) added

The basic structure of a facing arrangement with the focal point of leaves added

for the arrangement. Your commentary may run as follows: 'I like to suggest an approximate height for the tallest point, setting it three-quarters back in the vase. Then find two suitable stems for the sides, then perhaps two more, shorter than the first pieces, to go in between these points and leaning back slightly so that it makes a more all-round looking arrangement. Now I would suggest something right over the centre front. This links the vase with the flowers and stops the surprised look. It 'breaks' the hard rim of the vase. Now look at the middle of the vase. Get some more foliage and fill in a little, making the different foliages run in sweeps, bringing the varieties through the vase. Two or three different types are wanted here' (and so on).

Look at each stem for its curve and see that it flows properly. Every three or four pieces you add should be shown to the audience by turning the turntable

A plan of an outline structure for an all-round arrangement

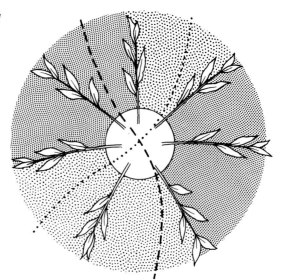

A side view of the basic structure for an all-round arrangement

A plan of an outline structure for an oval arrangement

A side view of the basic structure for an oval arrangement

around. I still cannot work from the back of the vase. Once the foliage is fixed, now start adding the flowers, one at a time. Again bring these through in sweeps of colour or shape. No two flowers the same length should be next to each other. Do not overcrowd – leave room for each to develop. Get some right down deep to add weight to the vase and come out well over the front and sides. Try to get flowers of all stages together using buds, half-open and fully-open deep down.

Keep turning your arrangement round showing each special point of interest. Finally add a few short pieces of foliages to hide the netting and tidy up the back of the vase. It will help if you get the thickest stems in first, leaving the thin, wirey stems to the last. Don't forget to add water to top up.

After doing a facing arrangement I would suggest you do an all-round one – this again taken in stages. I like to set five to seven points to the outline, then the centre. Work down from the centre with flowers of different lengths right down to the netting or Oasis. Come out to the point working back to the centre point – no two flowers the same length. Do this from each outside point, working the different flowers through the group. Add a little foliage deep down, coming right through the arrangement. Keep all the stems flowing from the centre point.

Discuss the merits of each vase as you do each arrangement, and the best flowers to use in it – colours and textures will all count. Display each completed vase making a picture with your staging, keeping something striking to the last.

A mixed-foliage arrangement is always worth doing. It surprises people just what can be done with different shapes and colours. A fruit and vegetable group is also a talking point. I like working with plants but this is heavy material to move around and I am very inclined to make a mess working with soil. I feel very strongly about encouraging and helping people so any tips or suggestions that make the subject easier for the audience to understand should be given. Say what and why you are doing a set thing. If a stem or branch occasionally slips or moves, this is a good thing. Pass it off by saying something, so that they see it can happen to anyone. At the end, recap the details, top up with water and say how much you have enjoyed demonstrating and that they have been a very good audience.

Useful addresses

For classes:

The Constance Spry Flower School
Winkfield Place
Winkfield
Windsor
Berkshire
SL4 4RN

For hand-made flowers:

Monique Register
48 Sandy Lane
Petersham
Surrey
TW10 7EL

Appendix: Organisation of special occasions

If you have been asked to supply the decorations for a special occasion such as a wedding, funeral or party, you will find tht it saves you a great deal of time and trouble to make a full list of the details and requirements. The following are some suggested 'forms' for setting out this information fully and clearly. You may wish to add your own ideas for information to be included, but these should cover most of the details you will need!

Wedding

NAME AND ADDRESS OF BRIDE .....   TELEPHONE NO: ....
....
....

COUNTRY ADDRESS
(if different from above)   TELEPHONE NO: ....
....
....
....

DATE OF WEDDING: ....   TIME: ....
ESTIMATE ADDRESS   ACCOUNT ADDRESS
....
....
....

DETAILS OF WEDDING FLOWERS   PRICES

Bride's Bouquet ....
Head-dress ....
Grown up Bridesmaids
– bouquets @ ....
– head-dresses @ ....
Children
– bouquets @ ....
– head-dresses @ ....
Buttonholes ....
Corsages ....
Any other instructions on flowers, e.g. handbag spray, etc.

....
Delivery Instructions ....
Delivery Charge ....   Delivery Time ....
Deposit to be paid to hold order.

DECORATIONS

Church

Church address in full together with Vicar's name
Tel. No: ....
Details of resident flower lady
Time of work: ....
Flowers for: ....
Altar
Chancel
Body of Church
Window Sills
Font
Vestry, etc.
Church vases or own
Any special notes – water supply, electrics, key collection, etc.
Use of Church plinths etc.

   Make a note of times of any services when you may not be able to work, if plinths and vases are on loan, and clearing up details.

Reception Area

Reception address ....
Tel. No: ....
Name of Caterer: ....
Contact name: ....
Time of arrival: ....

Details of decorations required:

                                                              Prices

Large groups ....
Top Table ....
Table Decorations: ....
Cake Top: ....
Cake Table: ....

To hiring and transport costs
(pedestals/vases)

   This may seem a lot of detail but if you have a special file, everything will be put on record in one place so that anyone may follow your instructions fully. It is a great mistake to carry knowledge in your head; if, for instance, you were unable to be present at the time, your colleagues would be quite lost.

Funeral

When one has a large funeral to deal with it is sense to have another form on the following lines:

Name of Account   Telephone No: ....
....
Name of the deceased
....
Date and time of funeral: ....
Church address or crematorium

....
....
Vicar in Charge: ....   Tel. No: ....
Undertaker's address ....   Tel. No: ....
Contact Name ....
Details of flowers ....
Coffin Cross (measurements from undertaker) ....
Card detail ....
Other wreaths including flower colour, shape and card details
....
....
....
Time to be delivered ....
Where to be delivered (home of funeral directors) ....
Any special instructions ....
....

Party

Name ....
Address ....
....
Tel. No: ....   Contact Name: ....
Details of decorations in order of rooms with colour, position, vase, etc.

Each box or bucket of flowers will be numbered to go with the room number.

Garlands
Length required
No. of loops and distance apart
No. of posies between loops and table corners
Table centres for buffet

Details of clearing

Account to be sent to: ....

Index